WHEN YOU COME HOME
By Nancy Cavin Pitts

Based on the World War II experiences of
Daphne Kelley Cavin,
first featured in Tom Brokaw's
The Greatest Generation.

Published by:

Christian Devotions Ministries

P. O. Box 6494

Kingsport, TN, 37663

www.christiandevotions.us

http://lighthousepublishingofthecarolinas.com

books@christiandevotions.us

Published in association with

Lighthouse Publishing of the Carolinas

When You Come Home

Cover Design by Jeffrey Holmes • www.loosepaintart.com

Interior Design by Behind the Gift. • www.behindthegift.com

"Daphne Cavin's poignant story of love, loss and sacrifice was one of the most memorable I encountered in writing *The Greatest Generation*. Her daughter now completes the story with this very heartfelt book."
— **Tom Brokaw**

"Daphne Cavin's story is perhaps the most memorable of all the stories I've been privileged to tell in my newspaper career. Daphne shared her memories and her scrapbook documenting her brief marriage to a soldier who was killed in action in southern France in 1944. I wrote her story in February 1998, and it took on a life of its own when Tom Brokaw's researchers discovered it and included it in the best-selling book, The Greatest Generation. Brokaw put Daphne on the NBC Nightly News several times and she became a symbol of the sacrifices made by war widows. Her daughter Nancy Cavin Pitts has done a wonderful job of fleshing out Daphne's poignant story in When You Come Home. It makes this war widow's story come alive in rich detail in ways that newspapers and television never could. Mrs. Pitts has given us the definitive portrait of a World War II war bride whose love was lost in the defense of freedom." — **John Flora**

When You Come Home

When you come home, come home once more to me.
It is unlikely dear that I shall be
Articulate. The words I've wanted so
To say, I'll try in vain to speak, I know;
I shall reach blindly for you, stricken dumb
With swift and aching joy when you come.

Or if my tongue find utterance at all
It will be commonplace and trivial.
But you will understand and, oh, once more,
I'll feel your hand laid lightly on my hair
As was your wont, smoothing it again
And yet again. You'll lift my face and then
We shall forget all else. You'll hold me fast.
When you come home, come home to me at last!

Author Unknown

Acknowledgments

My precious mother, Daphne Kelley Cavin, passed away in 2010 at the age of 90. She and my father, Marvin, were married for 24 years before the Lord called Dad home in 1975. They enjoyed a good marriage, so Mom seldom talked about her first love, Raymond Kelley. That is, until 1998, when *Indianapolis Star* reporter John Flora drove to Lebanon, Indiana, to take a look at Mom's thick, black scrapbook filled with memories of World War II and the young soldier that she loved. Under Mr. Flora's skillful guidance, Mom's memories took on voice as she described a time in her life that had previously been tucked away in a shroud of mystery. Daphne Cavin's love story quickly became known in Lebanon, then throughout Central Indiana and beyond.

Now my brothers, Oren and Loren, my sister Janie, and I wish to express our deep gratitude to the following men who introduced Mom's story to the world:

Nancy Cavin Pitts

John Flora for crafting several beautifully-written stories about our mother for *The Indianapolis Star*;

Tom Brokaw for coming to Indiana to interview Mom for *NBC Nightly News* and including her story in his best-selling book, *The Greatest Generation*;

Indianapolis Channel 13 news anchor **John Stehr** for putting together a touching interview which aired on the local evening news.

Mom's story, *When You Come Home*, is now complete. I wish to thank the following two writers who helped me shape the manuscript into a meaningful and touching story:
Bob Chenoweth, Mooresville, Indiana
Gail G. Pitts, Lebanon, Indiana

For adding the final editing touches to my book,
I want to thank:
Andrea Merrell, Travelers Rest, South Carolina

For their excellent research assistance,
I would like to thank:
Jamey Hickson, Lebanon Public Library, Lebanon, Indiana
Nina Clearman, Petal, Mississippi
Martha Corinne Quayle, Wickenburg, Arizona
Gerald & Bernice Obrecht, Sullivan, Illinois
Janie Cassell, Lebanon, Indiana

When You Come Home

A very special thank you to **A.C. and Katherine Clark** for opening their Cookeville, Tennessee home to me so I could interview them for my book.

A.C. and Raymond found themselves in the same platoon while serving in France. They became friends, and A.C. was with Raymond when he was mortally wounded. I believe God's hand prompted A.C. to read *The Greatest Generation* and realize that his friend's wife was the subject of a chapter. Thank you, A.C., for contacting NBC so you could share personal stories with Mom about Raymond's deployment in France. The visit granted her closure and comfort.

Thank you to my "first readers" :
Fern Miner, Joyce Woodard, Carla Terrill Gwinn and
Amy Hammerle. Your encouraging words after reading the first draft gave me hope that someday the book would stir hearts.

Thank you to the members of my book club:
**Regine Prewitt, Carmen Bracken, Alice Ortner, Carol Hahn,
Shari Dixon, Jana Salathe, Linda Obrecht, Pam McCleave** and
Sue Fallon.
We had great fun meeting together to review the book! Your well-thought-out ideas and suggestions were invaluable in adding the final touches to the manuscript.

I want to thank **Cindy Sproles** and **Eddie Jones**
from Christian Devotions Ministries.
You took a chance on an unknown and unpublished author, providing me the opportunity to share this story with others. I pray that this book will help benefit the mission of Christian Devotions.

Finally, I want to thank my wonderful husband Mark for all of his patience while I worked on my project. His love and support during the past several years has meant the world to me.

Prologue

Saturday Morning, June 22, 1996

The box was heavier than she expected. Nancy frowned as she pulled it from the top closet shelf. Suddenly the mysterious contents shifted, jerking it from her grasp. As the box hit the floor, its feeble cardboard seams ripped apart, spilling family photos and albums all across the worn carpet.

Nancy turned and surveyed the mess. She sighed and looked at her mother apologetically.

"Sorry, Mom. I'm sure we've got another box we can put this stuff in. Don't get up. I'll take care of it."

As soon as Nancy left the room, Daphne smiled and rose quickly from her rocker, stepping nearer to the scattered pieces of history. She'd have to hurry before Nancy saw her. The seventy-six-year-old woman lowered her five-foot frame ever so slowly to the floor. She was painfully trying to retrieve and stack the strewn photos when her youngest daughter returned with a carton that once held copier paper.

Daphne held her breath and waited for the reproof.

Nancy knelt down and started to scold, "Mom, I can take care of this," but just in time she recalled her mother's important stipulation for their shared housing: *I'll come live with you, but only if you let me help around the house. I just can't be a piece of furniture sitting around.*

Nancy gave her mother a hug and together, in silence, they gathered the photos.

Watching her mother steal a moment of remembrance as she relished each picture, Nancy wished this day weren't so busy. She wished she had more time to indulge the woman who had shaped her character.

Well, another day perhaps. There was so much to be done.

Would the memory books ever fit in the new box? It had been years since she looked at them, but even now she remembered which books held the color photos of her own family and which ones held images in sepia tones of long ago. The older books had allowed her to know her mother and father in their youth and meet strangers to her from family stories. She looked again at her mother and smiled with an unspoken promise. *Another day, Mom. Another day.*

The photo albums fit perfectly in the new box. All but one. In her mother's hands was a book Nancy did not recognize. Its black leather binding was cracked and faded, and on the cover was inscribed in faintest gold: *Raymond Kelley.*

Nancy absently brushed back a wisp of brown hair as she watched her mother's crippled arthritic fingers trace the letters. The older woman's green eyes grew misty with memory and Nancy saw the years fall away when she smiled.

As Daphne lovingly opened the book, a tear rolled down her wrinkled cheek.

"Nancy, this is my love story..."

MY ONLY SUNSHINE

1

Early Monday Evening, July 14, 1941

The old Chevrolet sedan crested the hill and brought the Indiana sun full into Daphne Abston's eyes. She lifted her hand to filter the glare and stared straight ahead, ignoring the wisps of red hair billowing across her glasses. Her green eyes watered as she turned to Mamie Ward, her best friend, behind the wheel. "How can you see to drive?"

"I don't need to see," Mamie said. "I could find my way to the Thistlewaite's house blindfolded." Mamie stuck out her chin. She closed her eyes momentarily and teased the wheel left and right.

"Mamie!" Daphne squealed as the car drifted off the edge of the road.

Mamie giggled and swerved the car back onto the smooth part of the gravel roadway.

Daphne felt her heart return to normal. "What put you in such a mischievous mood?" As she stared at her friend, suddenly she knew. "I'll bet there's someone special you're anxious to see at the party."

When You Come Home

Mamie edged her foot off the accelerator. "Oh, not really, Daphne. Just ready to get on with the evening, I guess."

Daphne scolded her friend gently. "Well, I'd sure like to get there in one piece."

Mamie laughed. "Relax, Daph. You'll be fine."

But Daphne didn't *feel* fine. Mamie had been late picking her up and even though the extra few minutes had allowed some additional time to freshen up, Daphne found herself pacing the floor long before Mamie pulled into the driveway. Arriving promptly meant getting there a little bit early, not sliding in a few minutes after the scheduled start time.

Daphne tried to watch the road again, wanting to make sure Mamie didn't send them careening across a cornfield. The sun's brightness was almost blinding, so Daphne closed her eyes. She tried to concentrate on pleasant diversions, like the heady scent of honeysuckle and the resonant memory of Nelson Eddy's voice from the old wooden tabletop radio next to her father's chair, crooning *When We Were So Happy in May*. But the honeysuckle soon faded and Nelson proved no match for the ting-pop-a-ting of pebbles ricocheting inside the car's fenders and the hot whipping breeze that was successful in undoing her hair. By now, it was a windblown mess, and that was no surprise to Daphne. Many times she had spent hours smoothing her hair into a trendy style, only to end up with a head full of rebellious curls.

The temperature was slow in receding from the low 90s and the high humidity level was typical for a July evening in Indiana. Looking down at her pink and gray striped dress, Daphne expected to see perspiration coming through. Thankfully, the dress still appeared dry, but she rolled down the window further, hoping the hot breeze would somehow keep her cool.

Oh well. Mamie said the partygoers would mostly be from her

Sunday school class and they wouldn't expect her to look like a magazine cover. Everyone there would be struggling with the heat too.

More than a dozen cars lined the long driveway leading to the Thistlewaite's two-story farmhouse. "Looks like a good turnout," Mamie said, maneuvering the car behind a dusty gray Plymouth and shutting off the motor. She turned to Daphne and hurried her words. "Just give me a minute." She pulled a square compact from her purse, opened it, and frowned at her reflection. "My rouge is still in place, but look at my hair!" Finding a brush buried in her purse, Mamie desperately tried to repair the damage.

Daphne took her hand off the door handle and assessed her friend. "Oh, you poor thing. We certainly can't leave this car until your hair is just perfect . . . like mine, you know." She laughed softly as she ran her hand through her own wind-blown curls. "Come on, Mamie. We're late and I'm hungry. Let's go." Daphne jumped out of the car and made her way around to Mamie's side. But Mamie continued primping.

Daphne leaned against the car's fender, exaggerating her impatience. Hand on hip, she rolled her eyes skyward, drumming her fingernails on the hood of the Chevy in annoying cadence. Mamie ignored the melodramatics and finished her beauty repair. Finally, she was ready to go.

Daphne heard her stomach growling. "You said there'd be food, Mamie. I don't smell anything and I'm starving. In fact," she paused dramatically, "I think I could eat a horse and chase its rider."

Mamie laughed as she shut her car door. "You sure do love to eat, Daphne." She surveyed her friend's trim figure. "But you don't gain an ounce. It's really annoying how thin you are." She sniffed at the empty air. "We're just upwind. But don't worry. Mrs. T always has tons of food. Just wait till you taste her blackberry pie."

The girls linked arms and quickened their pace, hurrying up the long driveway to the back yard. *Finally* the aroma of the refreshments reached Daphne and she urged her friend along.

But Mamie refused to hurry, zigzagging through the noisy crowd of thirty-some young people.

Daphne recognized many of the faces, and most of the rest looked somewhat familiar. She had probably seen them in Lebanon before, perhaps hanging out on the square near the Ione Beauty Shop where she worked.

Most of the partygoers were younger than she, but at twenty Daphne was often mistaken for a young teen herself. It was quite irritating. Men had it easy. All they had to do was forget to shave for a couple of days and they could appear to be more mature. A little stubble could add years to a boy on the verge of manhood. Yet it was hard for her to think of them as men. Stubble or no stubble, they would always be country *boys* to her.

Mamie patted Daphne's arm. "Let's eat."

A tempting array of goodies covered the long table. The girls helped themselves to ham sandwiches, spicy baked beans, and scrumptious triangles of Mrs. Thistlewaite's blackberry pie. Taking seats at the far end of a picnic table, they dug in. During the meal, Daphne began to relax and look around the sprawling back yard. Some of the kids were already starting to play croquet and Daphne looked forward to joining them after she finished eating. Mamie pointed out a few of her closest friends from church. "I'll introduce you to some of them after while." She took one last bite of baked beans and wiped her mouth with her napkin. "I think I'll head over and talk with Mrs. T for a few minutes.

Do you want me to wait for you, Daphne?"

"No, go ahead." Daphne downed a swig of lemonade and picked up her fork. "Right now, I want to enjoy every last bite of this pie. I'll see you later."

As Daphne finished her dessert, she glanced around, taking in all the new faces. But then her eyes locked with those of a tall, handsome young man with blonde hair. Daphne looked away for a few seconds, but her eyes were drawn back to him. *What an attractive man*! He returned her glance through fashionable wire-framed glasses. Hoping she appeared interesting, she pretended to be smiling at an imaginary friend just across the yard. When she looked back, he was gone. Had he really been looking her over or merely surveying the buffet table? Disappointed, Daphne sighed and rose from her chair, lemonade in hand. Who was this captivating stranger?

"Hi, I'm Raymond Kelley." As she spun to see who had come up behind her, Daphne's hand jerked. She watched helplessly as her lemonade flew into the air, splattering all over the front of Raymond's trousers.

"Oh, no," Daphne stuttered as she tried to apologize. "I'm so sorry!" And she *was* sorry. Such luck. Why did she have to be so clumsy tonight? It was then she realized how this man towered over her. *He must be a foot taller than me,* she thought.

"I just wanted to meet you face-to-face," he said with a smile. There was kindness and forgiveness in his tone. Her heart melted, even as the words she wanted to say froze in her throat.

He was laughing now. "Like I said, I'm Raymond Kelley."

Daphne was still speechless.

"Shall I just call you 'Mamie's friend?'"

Taking a deep breath, Daphne relaxed enough to say, "My name's

Daphne. Daphne Abston."

Raymond stood even taller and extended his hand. She lifted her free arm and checked to be sure her hair hadn't stood on end during this stressful episode. Then feeling a little silly for being so self-absorbed, she looked up at Raymond's face one more time. "Please forgive me for my clumsiness," she whispered.

Raymond eased his hand away and came to her verbal rescue. "Don't worry about it. I probably would have spilled something myself before the night was over." He grabbed a napkin, tucked a corner of it behind his belt, and flattened the rest of it against his lap. "There. Nobody has to know. With this heat, it'll dry in a few minutes."

Raymond put her at ease. Soon she forgot all about the shaky introduction. As her initial nervousness faded away, she peppered him with questions.

Daphne sipped her lemonade *carefully* this time. "Where do you live, Raymond?"

"Well, I work in Indianapolis, so during the week I stay there with my aunt and uncle."

"Do your folks live around here?"

"Uh-huh. Just north of Milledgeville, about four miles. So I'm only home on weekends." He grinned. "But if I hear about a party, like tonight, I want to be there." As Daphne took one last sip of her drink, Raymond became the interrogator. "Now, how about you, Daphne? Are you a local girl?"

"Oh, yes, I don't live far from here. Just southeast of Lebanon, two or three miles."

After a few more moments of small talk, Daphne became distracted by a young man on the other side of the fence waving his arms wildly. "Hey, Kelley, come here for a minute." Raymond held up his hand, gesturing that he was otherwise occupied, but the man was insistent. "C'mon, Deed, hurry up."

Deed? Before Daphne could ask him why the fellow had called him Deed, Raymond sighed, shrugged his broad shoulders, and stood. "Looks like I'm being summoned. We'll talk later, okay?"

As he started away, Daphne called after him, "Raymond, what about your...?"

Raymond stopped and looked down at his makeshift paper loin cloth. Pounding his chest like Tarzan, he winked and walked away.

2

Early Saturday Evening, July 19, 1941

Daphne leaned over the desk at the Ione Beauty Shop and checked her appointment book. It was ten minutes past six and Mrs. Hunsaker, her last appointment of a very long day, was late. Early this morning, her new white cotton uniform had been freshly starched and crisp-looking. Now, the ninety-plus degree temperature and the hot air blasting forth from the hairdryers had taken a toll, leaving the dress wrinkled and wilted. Daphne was tempted to sit down for a few moments to rest her aching feet, but knew if she did, Mrs. Hunsaker would probably walk in right then.

She looked up from the desk and out the window to the street. Leaning closer to the glass, Daphne looked first left, then right, hoping to see her customer approaching. No sign of her. Any hope of getting home early faded fast. Looking again, she caught sight, not of Mrs. Hunsaker, but of a man pacing as if imprisoned in an invisible box just outside the shop. *Oh my word,* Daphne thought. *That looks like Raymond Kelley. But what in the world would he be doing in front of a beauty shop?*

19

Just then the door to the salon opened, setting off the squealing of hinges and the clang of the cowbell attached to the door. Daphne turned quickly. Her customer had finally arrived.

"Good evening, Mrs. Hunsaker," Daphne said with a smile. "How are you tonight?"

"Hello, Daphne," replied the older woman quietly. "I'm all right, but I do apologize for being late. Time sure seems to get away from me these days."

"Oh, that's all right. Let's get you started." Daphne led the older woman over to the shampoo chair and draped a cape around her shoulders.

Geraldine Hunsaker was one of the few quiet customers who wasn't much for idle chit-chat. It was just as well, since Daphne could think of nothing but Raymond. She replayed in her mind again and again meeting him at the party and her conversation with Mamie Ward the next day.

"You and Raymond certainly hit it off last night," Mamie had said with a knowing grin. "I told Mom, 'You should have seen Kelley last night. He fell like a ton of bricks for Daphne.'"

Daphne remembered feeling a little embarrassed while trying to contain her delight. "Well," Daphne had said, "I thought he was a very handsome man." She wouldn't admit that it had taken her over an hour to fall asleep that night or that Raymond Kelley had waltzed through her dreams a time or two since then.

"So you really think he's interested?"

"Well, he *did* hang around you most of the evening."

A smile crossed Daphne's face even now as she worked the shampoo into Mrs. Hunsaker's silver hair. She was thinking about the rest of what her friend had told her, about how Mamie knew Raymond from church and from school at Pinnell, and Mamie had confirmed Daphne's first impression of the young man—that he *was* outgoing and popular, just as she guessed. Of all the guys at the picnic, Raymond was certainly the most desirable.

"I'll bet he comes to see you," Mamie had predicted.

As Daphne rinsed the shampoo from Mrs. Hunsaker's hair, she looked out the window again, leaning a little closer to get a wider view of the street. Just then, Raymond—it was definitely Raymond—crossed in front of the window.

Daphne lost her firm grip on the nozzle and warm water sprayed the ceiling and dripped down the window panes. After regaining control of the sprayer, she muttered, "Good heavens, if the window had been open, I would've soaked poor Raymond Kelley again."

"What's that, dear?"

"Oh, nothing, Mrs. Hunsaker. I'm so sorry," Daphne said. Absently dabbing at the woman's misted face with a hand towel, she stole another glance at the water streaking down the inside of the window. Outside, Raymond grinned at her. Another man she didn't recognize pointed her way and laughed hysterically.

Daphne huffed and turned her back on them. How dare they act like I'm a mannequin in a store window, she fumed. If Raymond Kelley wants to ask me out, he can telephone me or come by the house like a gentleman.

Daphne engaged Mrs. Hunsaker in conversation, whether the old woman wanted to chat or not—anything to keep Raymond and his comedian friend from distracting her.

After taking extra time with her customer and bidding her goodbye, Daphne was ready to leave. She cracked open the front door, peered outside into the encroaching darkness, and slipped out behind the backs of a small group of people on the sidewalk. She hurried down the block and around the corner to her father's old black Plymouth. As soon as the engine chugged to life, she shifted into gear and started home.

That will teach them, she thought. But before turning the corner, she glanced in the rear view mirror, wondering if Raymond was among those still loitering outside the shop. Unfortunately, darkness was falling, hiding Raymond—if he was still there—with it.

A couple of weeks later, Daphne was on her hands and knees scrubbing the flowery pattern of the yellow and cream-colored linoleum stretching across her bedroom floor. It was certainly not her favorite thing to do on a Sunday afternoon. But she had neglected her cleaning long enough, so despite the stifling early August heat, on this day nearing 90 degrees, she had started the chore soon after church.

She had twisted a soft green cotton scarf around her head like a bandana. As she rose up on her knees and repositioned her scarf to better absorb the relentless sweat, the sound of a car door slamming drew her attention to the window. It was Raymond. "Oh, no!" she exclaimed to the empty room. "I'm certainly not dressed for company." Her gaze traveled all the way down to her feet, and she tugged on the old white anklets bunched around her shoes.

She ran to the mirror, yanked the scarf from her head, and used it to dab at her forehead. One look in the mirror confirmed her worse suspicions. *I can't let Raymond see me like this.*

She groaned out loud. "What will I do with this hair? It looks like it got caught in a mousetrap." Wilted by the humidity, her unruly curls spiraled in every direction.

Once again, she looked a fright.

And Raymond was here.

Now.

It had been almost three weeks since the party and more than two weeks since she had intentionally eluded Raymond at the beauty shop. As time had passed, Daphne figured that perhaps he had mistaken her furtive escape as a sign she wasn't interested. So maybe he had lost interest himself.

"Of course he still likes you," Mamie insisted. "He just needs to break off a relationship with another girl first."

"Another girl?"

"Oh now, don't worry. It's not a serious courtship. Besides," Mamie had whispered, "a little bird told me he's quite taken with your red hair and petite build."

"Just plain skinny is more like it," Daphne had muttered and, despite Mamie's reassurance, the passing days had filled her with doubt. But now—*now*, of all times—Raymond was here, knocking at her door.

"I'll get it," she yelled to her parents, still frantically trying to tame her defiant curls. Giving up, she ran from her room and through the old house to the front door.

Raymond bent his tall frame down and peered through the front screen as she approached. He smiled. "Hi, Daphne."

Now I mustn't look too eager, Daphne reminded herself as she swung open the door, inviting him into the small living room. Normally the sparse furnishings of her parents' home didn't bother her, but today she was critically aware of the threadbare couch and chair. How she wished they could get rid of this old furniture and get some pieces that actually matched. But thanks to the Depression and the loss of their 98-acre farm, such an expenditure was out of the question.

Nonetheless, Daphne could feel Raymond's eyes on her, and she knew he was not thinking about furniture.

"Would you like to go for a ride?" he asked.

You'd better believe I would, was the reply that popped into her head. But instead she nodded and, with what she hoped was a casual smile, answered, "I'd love to . . . but first, let me introduce you to my parents."

Raymond followed her into the spacious country kitchen where the two older Abstons sat at the oilcloth covered table, the fat Sunday paper spread out between them.

"Mother and Dad, I'd like you to meet Raymond Kelley."

Maggie Abston wasn't one to make over people. The slender, silver-haired woman simply smiled and shook Raymond's large outstretched hand. Albert Abston stood, a smile transforming his thin face as it lifted the corners of his bushy mustache. "Nice to meet you, young fellow," he said, firmly grasping Raymond's hand.

"Nice to meet you too, Mr. and Mrs. Abston. I guess I should call you Reverend and Mrs. Abston, shouldn't I?"

Daphne didn't recall telling him that her father was a retired minister. So Raymond obviously had been checking up on her background.

Her father grinned. "No need to be so formal. The Lord knows us as Maggie and Albert, so if it's good enough for Him..." He studied the tall young man. "You got family around here, Raymond?"

"Yes sir. My folks are Guy and Leona Kelley. They live just north of Milledgeville in Harrison Township."

"Of course. Your family has lived in the area for many years, haven't they?"

Raymond nodded and he and Daphne sat at the table as the four of them chatted a little longer. Maggie offered Raymond a glass of iced tea, but he politely declined and looked over at Daphne as if signaling that it was time to leave.

"Raymond asked me to go for a ride."

"It's awfully warm outside," her father said, but with his subtle approval, she and Raymond headed for the car.

Easing his old black Chevrolet onto the gravel road, Raymond headed west on U.S. 52. The winding road stretched for miles, and when they started out in silence, Daphne was tempted to ask Raymond what he and his friend were doing outside the salon that night. And she *really* wanted to know all about the girl he had broken up with.

Instead, she felt relief when Raymond had questions about her family. Despite the sweltering heat, she grew more comfortable as she told him how her father was already a fifty-year-old grandpa by the time she was born, and he still farmed thirty acres of leased land today with his workhorses, Pet and Daisy. She explained how her mother had given birth to ten children, although just seven survived to adulthood. Five boys came first. Sadly, two of them died shortly after birth. Then five little girls joined the family. Daphne was the youngest.

"When Mother was expecting me," she said, "my sister Margaret Jean died from Scarlet Fever. She was only eighteen months old. Then just two years ago, my oldest sister, Ruby, died during emergency gall bladder surgery."

"Oh, how awful," said Raymond. "How old was she?"

"Barely thirty. She was more like a mother to me than a sister. She always seemed content to stay at home and help Mother and Dad. Her death left a big hole in all our lives. Ruby was ten years old when I was born, and even then she was an amazing seamstress. Mother said Ruby sewed most of my baby clothes." Daphne paused thoughtfully. "Ruby taught me all the things a proper country girl needs to know."

"What kind of things?"

"Oh, you know, how to hitch a horse to the plow without getting squashed by an oversized hoof, how to gather eggs without being attacked by flying hens, and how to aim the 'spigots' when milking a cow, and..."

Daphne thought of the wild water-spray incident at the salon and turned toward Raymond. His smirk belied that he was thinking the same thing. They smiled together.

"Essential information, all of it," Raymond agreed.

Then Daphne told him about her brothers. Chester, Jim, and Orville had long since moved away from the area. "Chester was married before I was even born. His wife, Agnes, gave birth to a little boy when I was just fifteen months old. Unfortunately, when little Jack was only eight-months-old, his parents separated and divorced."

"Oh, really? That must have been hard for your family."

"You can't imagine. Filing for divorce in the early twenties was considered quite disgraceful, especially for a preacher's son. I think it hurt Dad more than anyone else. Anyway, neither Chester nor Agnes was financially stable at the time, so Jack came to live at our house. Since he was so close to my age, he was more like a brother to me than a nephew. He called my folks Mom and Dad and for some strange reason, even though he could talk plain as could be, he called me Daphna, never Daphne."

"Daphna?"

She nodded. "Just his special way of pronouncing my name, I guess. Jack's always been a rascal."

Raymond glanced at Daphne. "I'll bet he's not the only rascal in the family. You have sort of a mischievous look about you too, Miss Daphne."

"Why, Mr. Kelley, I don't know what you mean," she said, feeling color rising in her cheeks.

"Okay, okay, so you're a perfect angel. But tell me, did that little devil Jack ever get you into any trouble?"

Daphne gave Raymond a long look. She wasn't certain it was wise on their first date to talk about her "childhood escapades." But she felt so comfortable with this man. Despite the lemonade mishap at the party, the surprise rain-shower at the beauty parlor, and her messy red hair, Raymond obviously found her company to his liking.

"Jack and I had our moments," she began. "I remember one summer day when we were about five and six. I guess we got a little overheated from playing cowboys and Indians around the barn lot and we decided a cool dip would feel pretty good. So we took off our clothes and jumped into the horse tank. It didn't occur to us, or maybe we just didn't care, that our little water hole was in full view of the road in front of the house.

"Mother and Dad were sitting on the porch enjoying the warm sunshine, quite oblivious to our shenanigans just a few yards away. But my Aunt Ellie across the road got quite an eyeful. I can still hear her yelling as she came charging across the yard. 'Maggie Abston, look at what those kids of yours are doing!'"

Raymond laughed. "Typical preacher's kids, huh?"

Daphne told Raymond about her sisters Ruth and Bernice, and how they, too, had married and left Lebanon. Ruth moved to Illinois and Bernice to the north side of Indianapolis. "Neither of my sisters has children yet, although I'm sure they would both welcome the patter of little feet." Daphne paused then, suddenly realizing that describing a family of twelve had taken them a long way from home. She turned to Raymond as he drove. "Now you tell me about your family, Raymond."

"Okay, but not until I find out more about you, Daphne. Like, how long have you worked at the Ione?" Raymond's eyes turned serious. "And what do you want to do with your life?"

Daphne thought back. "Well, I started working for Ione Davidson right after beauty college, so I've been there a couple of years now. The time has really gone by fast. I enjoy cutting and styling hair and getting to know my customers, but the hours are long. Mrs. Davidson expects us to stay late most evenings and we have to work every Saturday."

Raymond turned and smiled. "I think your customers are lucky to have you."

"Thank you, sir. I would really love to own and operate my own beauty shop some day. But I wouldn't ask my employees to work late *every* night, and I'd also make sure they had a Saturday off now and then."

Raymond chuckled softly.

"Now I want to hear about you, Raymond."

Raymond described his two brothers and two sisters. "Floyd is two years older than me. Just last year, he married Twyla and they live on a farm south of Lebanon. Then there's Mary, who is two years younger than me. She still lives at home. Delmar is next. He's three years younger than Mary and in the eighth grade. And last, but not least, is Frances, who's only nine. She's a real sweetie and follows me around the house whenever I'm home."

"My father is a farmer, but farming holds no interest for me. I've been working at Kingan Meats in Indianapolis for about a year now."

"The slaughterhouse in Indianapolis?"

Raymond quickly glanced over, obviously to assess her reaction, then nodded.

Disturbing visions of upside down carcasses, buckets of animal parts, and lots and lots of blood floated around Daphne's brain like a cheap horror movie. What should she say next? She had more questions, but they might be better left unsaid. She asked anyway. "What do you do there?"

"I operate a meat grinder. You know, for making hamburger, sausage, and hot dogs."

"Oh. That's not too gruesome. But isn't the smell pretty awful, even with the windows cranked opened?"

His eyes and expression told the story. "I guess I've just learned to put the sights and the smells out of my mind."

"I'll bet your mother has a hard time with your laundry."

He chuckled. "No, the company provides a uniform each day after we clock in. When our shift is over, we shower and wear our street clothes home."

"That's definitely a good thing," Daphne smirked cheerfully as she cranked her window down another two inches coaxing more air inside the car. "Kingan must be a really large operation."

Raymond nodded. "Yes. I think it's the fifth or sixth largest meat packing company in the country." He stretched his left arm out the car window to signal a left turn and then glanced at Daphne. "It's not the job I want to keep forever, but right now it helps bring in extra money to help my folks."

Daphne turned and studied Raymond's strong, kind face. "So what *would* you like to do with your life, Raymond? Once the economy gets better and you don't have to help out your folks, I mean."

"Oh, I'll probably always be helping somebody out," he laughed. "That's just the way I am, I guess. It sort of annoys my friends, actually."

"Does that have anything to do with why they call you 'Deed?'"

Raymond rolled his eyes. "Yeah, it started out as 'Good Deed Kelley.' Kind of a joke at first, and I guess it could be worse. Anyway, now I'm stuck with it."

"I think it's nice," Daphne said.

Raymond glanced over at her and gave her a wink. After a brief silence, he said, "I guess it's a nickname I can live with even if I become a minister someday."

Daphne's eyes opened wide. She was surprised. "The Reverend Deed Kelley. Has a nice ring to it. Do you feel called to enter the ministry?"

He nodded, but didn't elaborate. "As long as I could still lead singing for the congregation like I often do now."

Daphne somehow knew that Raymond would have a fine singing voice since his speaking voice was so deep and rich. She was tempted to ask him to sing a song for her, but she was afraid he might ask her to sing too. And she didn't want to scare him off.

Besides, all too soon they were pulling back into her driveway.

Raymond held her hand as he escorted her to the front door. "Can I take you out again, Daphne?"

Thrilled, she looked up at him and nodded, wishing time would stand still. Before Daphne could say anything, Raymond bent down and brushed his lips against hers. He bid her good night and ambled confidently down the steps into the dark.

What a guy, Daphne thought as she watched him drive away. She touched her lips and ached for him to kiss her again. Maybe a handshake would have been more customary and proper, but his boldness made her heart pound wildly.

Inside the house, she crossed in front of her father who was sprawled in his favorite chair, reading. "How was your drive, honey?"

"He was nice, Dad." Daphne saw her father's quizzical look and turned to fully face him. "I mean *it* was nice. It was a real pleasant drive."

She wandered into the kitchen, opened the ice box, pulled out the pitcher, and poured a glass of tea. Noticing the calendar just above the ice box, Daphne picked up her mother's yellow crossword pencil from

When You Come Home

the table and circled the date: August 3, 1941.

It was a very good day.

3

Early Saturday Evening, August 16, 1941

After sharing a dish of ice cream at the Guernsey Milk and Ice Cream Company—chocolate for Raymond and orange-pineapple for Daphne—the new couple hurried to the Avon Theater on the Lebanon town square. They were meeting Mamie Ward and her new boyfriend, Jim Gates, to take in the movie, *Hit the Road*. Daphne knew little about the film, but she really didn't care what it was about. This would be her first movie with Raymond and that was all that mattered.

The August heat subsided as nightfall approached, but it was still uncomfortable just standing around waiting for Mamie and Jim, so Daphne and Raymond decided to walk around the square. Raymond's manners were exemplary, and he took the manly protective position by the curb. Just being with Raymond made the familiar route seem even more special. After turning the corner, the couple headed south on Lebanon Street. They passed Wheeler's Café and Star Drug Store, two of Daphne's lunchtime hangouts. Turning onto Main Street, they walked by another of Daphne's favorite places, Kate's Confectionery. All of these establishments were conveniently close to the Ione salon. Since she could eat or drink practically anything and never gain an ounce, Daphne knew the delights of these establishments well.

She looked up at Raymond as they walked along and couldn't help noticing how stately the Boone County courthouse looked over his shoulder. She had seen the grand concrete and limestone structure hundreds of times, but for some reason it seemed particularly majestic this night. But when Raymond took her hand in his, Daphne forgot all about the backdrop of the courthouse. Suddenly only his touch mattered. Only his presence seemed majestic.

Turning north onto Meridian Street, the couple was just passing the J.C. Penney store when a voice yelled, "Daphna! Hey Daphna, wait up!"

Releasing Raymond's hand, Daphne turned and spread her arms wide. Jack Abston rushed up and she gave him a long hug. Stepping back, she looked at him and then hugged him again. Her nephew had matured into a handsome young man. His black wavy hair and deep blue eyes were set off by a quick and mischievous grin. Daphne didn't dare tell him she thought he rather resembled a young Frank Sinatra.

"Jack, this is Raymond. Raymond, you remember I've told you about Jack."

The two men nodded and shook hands.

Daphne smiled warmly at her nephew. "Jack, I haven't seen you for weeks. You look great."

"Must be that cosmopolitan living in the grand metropolis of Muncie," he said. "So, Mom said the two of you were off to the Biograph."

"The Biograph?" Raymond looked puzzled.

"Oh, don't pay any attention to him, Raymond," Daphne chided.

"Even when the Avon was called the Colonial Theater, Jack decided he would call it the Biograph. He's always changing the names of things. And people."

"Wasn't the Biograph the name of the theater where John Dillinger was killed?"

Jack put his hands on his hips in mock disbelief. "C'mon, Daphna, didn't you tell Raymond about our encounter with the infamous John Dillinger?"

Raymond looked back and forth between the two of them until finally Daphne said, "There are lots of things I haven't told Raymond yet, Jack."

Seizing the center-stage opportunity, Jack began. "Well Raymond, it was...let's see, back in '34, I suppose. Anyway, there we were, thirteen or fourteen years old, sitting on the porch one hot summer morning when..." Jack paused for effect. It worked, because Raymond stepped closer.

But instead of continuing his story, Jack shook his head. "Well, listen, you probably need to get going, so I won't keep you." He extended his hand. "Raymond, it was nice to meet—"

"Oh no you don't, Jack. What about Dillinger?"

As if on cue, Jack continued . . . "Well, if you insist." He winked at Daphne. "To begin with, you have to understand that Mom always believed in feeding any poor, hungry soul who stopped by the house looking for a handout. If Daphna and I were outside, we might catch sight of some scroungy looking man heading up the driveway. We'd yell, 'Mom, here comes another tramp!' and by the time the fellow would get to the house, Mom would already be out on the front porch, telling him to stay put while she got him something to eat."

They began walking again and Daphne picked up the story. "Jack and I would run inside while Mother fixed a plate of hot food. But we'd peek out the curtains just to be sure our visitor didn't make off with anything."

Jack continued. "Well, one day this man in a rumpled suit was already on the porch when we came around the side of the house. Now remember, this was around the time John Dillinger was on the loose and running from the law. In fact, it was rumored that he was heading for Chicago, so Boone County was right in his path. He was already knocking on the door when we first saw him, so there he was between us and Mom, who was on the inside of the screen door. Even after she went into the kitchen to dish up some food, the man stayed by the door, almost like he didn't want us to go in. And the longer I looked at his face, the more certain I was it was Dillinger."

"Then what happened?" Raymond asked.

Jack laughed. "Well, let me tell you, my knobby knees were shaking so much they sounded like a fife and drum corp without any fifes. Anyway, it was real awkward. The three of us just stood there. Nobody said a word. So when the man turned away for a minute, I grabbed Daphna and pulled her around the side of the house."

"I think I still have the bruises," Daphne cut in.

"So I yanked her out of sight and whispered, 'Daphna, I think that's John Dillinger.' Well, let me tell you, her eyes nearly popped out of her head."

"You were scared too, Jack."

Jack lowered his voice as they reached the theater and several people passed by. "Well, we had a right to be frightened. We were thinking that at any time, this Dillinger guy might pull out a gun and shoot all of us. We were just about to high-tail it for the back door when Mom came out and handed the man a plate of food."

"You should have seen him eat." Daphne shook her head at the memory. "We figured being 'on the lam' must make a fellow pretty hungry."

"Mom couldn't get him to talk much, but as soon as he left, we flew into the house yelling, 'Mom, that guy was John Dillinger!'"

Daphne took Raymond's hand, drawing his eyes away from Jack. "Mother said our imagination was getting the best of us."

"Yeah," Jack said, shaking his head, "but you know, I always felt sure it was him. And a few weeks later we heard the FBI had gunned down Dillinger in front of the Biograph."

"Well," said Raymond. "Whether it was him or not, I'm sure it was quite an adventure for you both." After a moment he added, "Jack, why don't you come to the show with us?" He looked down at Daphne and squeezed her hand. "You wouldn't mind, would you, Daphne?"

Pleased that Raymond had taken a liking to her nephew, she seconded the idea. "Of course not. Come on, Jack."

"Thanks anyway. I'd love to, but I really just came to town to give Daphna a birthday kiss." He leaned close to Daphne and gave her a peck on the cheek. Stepping back, he seemed to notice a sudden look of concern on Raymond's face. "Don't worry, Raymond," Jack said, "I think you'll be safe at the Biograph. After all, your lady's not wearing red. And unless you're really Machine Gun Kelley escaped from prison, I don't think the FBI will show up tonight."

Raymond smiled, but still seemed distracted.

"Happy birthday, kid," Jack said again. "Have fun at the movie. I need to hit the road."

Hit the Road turned out to be a "B" movie of the highest order, an odd film about kids setting out for revenge after their fathers were murdered in a mob war. What bothered Daphne most was that the film played it for laughs. The plot was populated by characters with funny names like Pig, String, Ape, Pesky, and Patience. But there was nothing humorous about murder and revenge, Daphne thought. Then again, maybe she wasn't seeing the humor in it because her mind kept drifting. Maybe she couldn't stomach the newsreel footage of Germany's invasion of Russia. But more likely, she knew she was simply worried about Raymond. After their encounter with Jack, Raymond seemed to grow tense and fidgety. Upon reflection, Daphne realized his demeanor had changed after Jack mentioned it was her birthday.

Though she had planned to invite Raymond over for cake after church the next day, she hadn't mentioned it yet. It was so early in their courtship it seemed awkward to say, "Hey, it's my birthday." Now it occurred to her that maybe she should have found a way to let him know.

About twenty minutes into the show, Raymond leaned over and whispered, "I'm going to the . . . um . . . well, I'll be right back."

Daphne nodded and took the popcorn from him as Raymond crouched down and crossed before her and their friends. She tried to concentrate on the film, but kept finding herself paying attention to it only when Mamie would laugh at something and by then the joke was over.

As the moments passed without Raymond's return, Daphne grew more concerned. She set the popcorn down on his empty seat and turned to survey the exit. He had been gone too long.

Mamie and Jim both laughed, drawing Daphne's eyes back to the screen. She ate more popcorn, one kernel at a time so there would be some left for Raymond when he returned—*if* he returned.

After what seemed an eternity, even Mamie noticed. "What's keeping

Raymond?" she whispered. Daphne just shrugged and tried to hide her panic. She knew she was wavering between being a little put out with him for leaving her alone so long and being genuinely concerned about him. What if he was sick?

Finally in desperation, Daphne leaned over to Mamie, "Would you ask Jim to go check on Raymond?"

Mamie turned and whispered to Jim, but just as he started to get up, light from the lobby filtered into the theater and Daphne turned to see Raymond returning to his seat.

"Sorry," he said as he sat down. He handed Daphne the box from his seat, apparently unaware she had already eaten most of it. Since he had come back seeming whole and hearty, Daphne's concern gave way to disappointment. It was very rude, she thought, for him to have left her alone in the theater for nearly fifteen minutes with not so much as a word of explanation.

Soon enough, *Hit the Road* was over. Because Mamie had to prepare for Sunday school the next morning, she and Jim quickly took their leave. As Daphne watched them exit the theater, she noticed the girl behind the candy counter trying to make eye contact with Raymond. Though Raymond paid no attention, Daphne sullenly wondered if the candy-girl was the reason Raymond had been gone so long. Could she be his old girlfriend?

Well, she wasn't about to let Raymond "Good Deed" Kelley or anyone else treat her like that. So when Raymond tried to hold her hand again on the way to the car, she pulled away. "I'm sleepy," she insisted, pretending to cover a yawn.

"Are you okay, Daphne?"

She gave him a fake little smile. She would be civil even though it would probably be her last date with Raymond. "Just tired, I guess."

When You Come Home

They walked in silence to the other side of the square where Raymond's Chevy was parked. After opening the door for Daphne, Raymond walked around and got behind the wheel. He turned to her and started to say something just as she planned to tell him that maybe they shouldn't see each other again. But their words jumbled together until they paused, then simultaneously said, "What? You go first."

They laughed and Daphne said, "You first, Raymond. I insist."

"Okay," he said as he reached into his pocket and pulled out a candy box. "I didn't know it was your birthday, Daphne. I'm sorry. I wish I had known. I had a rough time figuring out something I could give you on such short notice. But I like a challenge, so I do have a gift for you."

He handed her the box. "This isn't much of anything. It's kind of silly, really."

Daphne opened the flap on the box and pulled out strands of licorice onto which Raymond had strung Lifesavers candy. "It's a necklace," Raymond said. "I mean, you know, a beautiful girl like you deserves jewelry on her birthday."

Daphne's involuntary smile of relief happened so quickly she wasn't sure if she would burst out laughing or dissolve into tears. Instead, she leaned over and kissed Raymond on the cheek, then hugged him long and hard. When she finally released him, he said, "Oh, wait a minute, there's more," and he reached back into his pocket. He handed her a partial roll of Lifesavers. "I saved the orange and pineapple ones so you could eat them right away." Then he handed her two movie tickets, still whole and bound together at the perforation. "It's a card," he said. "Open it."

Daphne leaned forward under the glow of a streetlight and read the inscription inside the tiny tickets: Sweets for a Sweetheart. Happy Birthday, Daphne. Raymond.

Now she knew why the candy-counter girl had been staring at Raymond. She had probably never met such a wonderful man in her life.

Raymond helped her put on the candy necklace. "I hope this doesn't melt and mess up your dress," he said. But Daphne wasn't worried about the candy.

The only thing melting was her heart.

4

Autumn, 1941

S oon Daphne and Raymond were spending every weekend together. On Saturday afternoons during autumn, Raymond played basketball and, whenever she could, Daphne was there to cheer him on. Afterward, she would accompany him to his parents' house so he could wash up before they spent the evening together. While waiting for Raymond to get ready, Daphne would often sit in the kitchen of the Kelleys' white, wood-frame, two-story country home. There she would chat with Raymond's parents, sometimes helping Leona snap fresh green beans while sipping a glass of tea.

Daphne grew fond of Leona. A pleasant woman, she had a big heart and delightful sense of humor. She thrived in her role as mother of five, and Daphne was touched by the playful, warm affection between Raymond and his mother.

Guy Kelley was likable too, though reserved. A hard worker, he struggled to make ends meet for the family and seemed humbled even more by the fact that Raymond helped out by giving his parents a portion of his weekly earnings.

Barely into his teens, Delmar seemed quite awkward and Daphne could already tell he would mature into a shy man like his father. Nine-year-old Frances was a different story. The cute little blonde had energy and infectious charm beyond even that of her mother and Raymond.

Daphne had also spent some time with Raymond's other sister, Mary, and looked forward to becoming closer to her. Mary adored Raymond. Being younger, she looked up to him and Raymond always seemed to make time for her.

Raymond was becoming a frequent guest at Daphne's home as well and had developed a warm relationship with her parents, Maggie and Albert. Daphne's sisters, too, had become fond of Raymond and often teased their kid sister about her boyfriend. "This one must be different, Daphne," Bernice had said. "You usually don't take any boy seriously for this long. Always before, you were finished with one and ready to move on to the next before we even got an introduction."

Daphne could only smile when Ruth said, "Oh honey, it's obvious he's as crazy about you as you are about him."

Around the beginning of November, Daphne's older brother Orville, his wife Mildred, their toddler son Ralph, and baby Larry Earl, arrived from Kansas for a six-day visit. In anticipation of their visit, Daphne had scheduled a few days off work, and was enjoying every minute of her vacation. She and her parents joined Orville's family as they traveled around the county, visiting relatives, reacquainting themselves with old friends, and distributing flowers at family gravesites. Raymond spent time with them too, and seemed as taken as she was with well-behaved Ralph and baby Larry.

On one Friday evening, Earl, Ruth, Clarence, and Bernice arrived to welcome the out-of-state relatives. Dinner was ready to be set on the table and Raymond had been invited to stay. Daphne felt her anticipation rise. It was important the evening was a success.

Ruth passed a platter of fried chicken to her brother. "How was your trip, Orville? Did you meet up with any bad weather?"

"It rained off and on, but no snow or ice, thank goodness," Orville said as he hunted for a drumstick and handed the plate to Earl. "That ten-hour drive sure is a long one."

Mildred agreed. "Especially with a wiggly little boy and a baby who refused to nap."

Raymond looked across the table at little Ralph. "Was that you turning somersaults in the front yard this afternoon?"

Ralph's eyes lit up as he nodded his head. "Uh-huh." He grinned shyly. "Do it again?"

Raymond smiled into the little boy's eager face. "Maybe later. Are you going to teach your little brother how to do flips when he gets older?"

Ralph looked puzzled. "No. He's a baby."

Bernice shared a smile with Daphne.

Mildred began spoon-feeding Larry. "Ralph, your brother won't always be little."

Pounding his chubby fists on the table, Larry's brown eyes sparkled. Suddenly the baby's fast-moving hands collided with a spoonful of mashed peas headed his way. Green globs flew everywhere, across the table top, into Daphne's half-filled coffee cup, and even on the front of Raymond's shirt.

"Yuck!" Ralph's face contorted as he surveyed the food disaster. Laughter erupted around the table and the aunts and uncles seated nearby hastily grabbed napkins and began helping Mildred clean up. Before her date could lift a hand, Daphne leaned over and wiped his shirt. "So how many children do you expect to have someday, Mr. Kelley?" she murmured.

Unruffled, Raymond looked into her eyes. "Oh, ten or twelve at least, give or take a few, Miss Abston."

Late on a Saturday afternoon in early December, Daphne left work early and made a quick trip to Adler's dress shop. Now, standing before the oval wall mirror in her bedroom, she turned from side to side, admiring the new black skirt. Feeling like a model, Daphne was excited about her purchase. She couldn't wait to show Raymond.

The fluttering of fabric, however, had chilled her legs in the cool room, so she went to her dresser, gave an affectionate little touch to the candy necklace hanging from one of the knobs, and opened the drawer. She pulled out her old pink cotton "snuggies." Though made for women, Daphne thought the knee-length underwear less than feminine. But the chill of early December had settled in, so she put on the ugly old things, adjusting them under her skirt until the brightly colored undergarment was hidden beneath the black material.

As she checked her rouge, another flash of color caught Daphne's eye, this one outside her bedroom window. In the fall of 1941, the foliage of Lebanon had abandoned its show of color all too quickly. For well over a month now the trees had stood naked, rendering the landscape stark and barren. Shades of gray were all that remained outside Daphne's window, except for an aqua-colored car pulling into their driveway.

When the car came to a stop and the gravel dust blew past it, the driver stepped out. It was Raymond.

Daphne slipped on her shoes and raced into the living room. Meeting Raymond at the door, she said, "Whose car is that?"

Raymond stared at her through the screen. "Hello to you too. May I come in?"

"Oh, of course." Daphne stepped aside and followed Raymond into the living room. She cocked her head to get a good look at his face as she took his coat, but Raymond avoided her gaze.

"How are you doing today, Reverend Abston?"

Albert Abston placed the *Reader's Digest* face down on his lap and shot a scolding look over the top of his glasses at the young visitor.

Raymond corrected himself. "Albert, I mean."

"I'm doing just fine, Raymond, thank you very much."

Daphne was practically bouncing up and down, anxious for her question to be answered. Waiting until Albert picked up his magazine and again started thumbing through the pages, Raymond leaned down and gave Daphne a quick kiss.

She pulled away from him. "The car?"

"Oh, that. Well the owner's letting me take it out for a spin."

"Who's the owner?"

"Just some ol' guy they call 'Deed'."

"You bought a new car?" Before Raymond could say another word, Daphne ran from the house, slipping into his coat as she bounded from the porch.

A few moments later, after Daphne had already circled the car twice, Raymond calmly caught up to her. He held out her coat. "I think this might be a little small for me. Want to trade?" Daphne laughed and gave Raymond his own coat.

"It's a Ford Deluxe," he said as Daphne ran her fingers over the coupe's sleek fenders and down a tear-drop headlight. "Not brand new, of course; it's a '39."

Daphne circled the car, but stopped to trace the outline of the rumble seat. She looked at Raymond—laughed when he nodded and winked—then continued on. She opened the passenger door and climbed in. "It's got a radio."

"A six-tube," Raymond added.

"Oh, Raymond, it's just beautiful, inside and out."

"No," he said, "it's just a car. You're beautiful, inside and out." He opened the driver's door, slid behind the steering wheel, and leaned toward her. They kissed—a tender, sweet kiss that stole their misty breaths from the chilled air. As they drew apart, Daphne shyly looked down, and when the mist of her breath parted, she caught a glimpse of pink cotton. Quickly, she smoothed out her black skirt to cover the snuggies. She looked back to Raymond. "Take me for a drive."

"Shouldn't I at least say hello to your mother?"

"Just a short drive. Mother will understand."

Raymond nodded and turned the ignition key. The motor rumbled smooth and rich. Once on the road, the coupe hummed along through the countryside. Daphne started playing with the radio buttons. Between the big band music and static, news of the escalating tensions in Europe seemed to dominate the airwaves. She glanced at Raymond. He had grown quiet, his look somber as he listened to the war talk. He caught her eye. "Will you shut that off please, sweetheart?"

Daphne turned off the radio and leaned her head against Raymond's shoulder as he turned the car around. When they got back to the house, Daphne asked him to go on inside. "I'll be there in a minute or two," she promised.

As Raymond headed for the front porch, Daphne scuttled around to the back of the house. The outdoor privy was a drafty little wood building, so cold weather demanded quicker business there. Running back to the house, she passed her father, who was bundled up for a trip to the barn to feed his beloved chestnut horses.

After washing her hands at the black-handled pump in the back room, Daphne rushed in through the kitchen, throwing off her coat as she strode into the living room. Still cold, she jumped about to warm herself and then circled slowly around Raymond, making sure he noticed her new skirt. Raymond's eyes sparkled as he tried to catch her hand, but missed. Daphne flirted teasingly as she stole away from his grasp and waltzed into the kitchen to make some fresh lemonade.

Maggie was carefully removing a tray of melted ice water from underneath the icebox. As she stood up, the water-filled metal container wobbled in her hands. "Daphne, I noticed the block of ice is really melting. The ice man should be coming tomorrow, but if he doesn't, please help me remember to send your dad to town to get another block. I laid fifteen cents on the table by the door in case he comes and I'm not here."

Daphne removed an ice pick from the drawer and grabbed an empty pitcher. Then she walked over to the old wooden ice box and pulled open the bottom compartment, which held the dwindling block of ice. "Oh my. There isn't much left, but I just need a few chunks." She attacked the ice with a pick, chipping off just enough to cover the bottom of the pitcher, which she carried to the counter. Reaching up to the windowsill to select some ripe lemons, Daphne looked over at her mother. Maggie was trying not to smile. "Daphne, dear," she said, "you're wearing your pink snuggies today, aren't you?"

Daphne frowned slightly, set the lemons on the counter, then smoothed the front of her skirt down, trying to cover whatever snippet of pink might be showing.

"I think you might want to..."

Albert came back into the house, looked toward Daphne, and started laughing.

"What's so funny?" Daphne asked, but as soon as she said it, she felt the rush of cold air against her bottom. "Oh my heavens," she said, frantically tugging her skirt back into place. She could feel her face turning pink, and she imagined it was a far deeper pink than her snuggies.

Over her father's waning laughter, she moaned, "Oh, Mother, Raymond must have seen my long underwear all the way up my backside."

Maggie laughed and touched her daughter's hand. "He probably didn't notice, dear. You know how unobservant men can be."

Albert started laughing again.

That night after Raymond was gone and she was ready for bed, Daphne walked back into the kitchen. She pulled the pitcher of lemonade from the icebox and poured a small glass. As she sat alone at the table and drank the cool liquid, she looked out the window. Nightfall had blacked out the world, and Daphne closed her eyes to remember the true colors of the day. She thought about Raymond's new blue-green car. It was bright and beautiful, but no more so than Raymond's light blue eyes. She thought about the snuggies incident. Her own face must have turned shades of red, but the shocking pink snuggies hadn't shocked Raymond at all. She opened her eyes and clamped a hand to her mouth. Then she burst into giggles. When she had settled down enough not to choke on her drink, she finished her lemonade. Picking up the crossword pencil, she went back to the icebox and marked another day off the calendar. December 6, 1941, had been a good day, full of color.

All her days were good since meeting Raymond Kelley.

She was certain tomorrow would be no different.

When You Come Home

5

Sunday Morning, December 7, 1941

❝ ...and we ask thee also, oh Lord, to bless the world outside these walls with that perfect peace that comes from knowing you as those of us inside this sanctuary surely do. This is our prayer in the name of our precious Lord and Savior, Jesus Christ. Amen.❞

The Reverend J.C. Coons lifted his head slowly and surveyed the congregation in the little Milledgeville Methodist Church. The preacher's calm demeanor reminded Daphne of her father's comforting delivery before he had retired from the pulpit. As she worshipped next to Raymond and his family, Daphne was certain her parents would enjoy visiting the Kelley's home church someday. She liked Milledgeville Methodist; liked its smallness, its homey, country character. And she appreciated how the congregation had made her feel welcome from the moment Raymond had ushered her into their midst a couple of months earlier. The little white country church had become her second church home, just as the Kelleys had become almost like a second family.

The Reverend smiled down at the third row. "And now, Brother

Kelley, would you once again lead our song service?"

Raymond nodded and stood, giving Daphne's hand a squeeze as he stepped into the center aisle. Nine-year-old Frances, his baby sister, sitting to Daphne's left, had already opened the hymnal to *What a Friend We Have in Jesus.* As she slid the book over to share with Daphne, the little girl rolled her eyes and whispered, "I wonder what song he'll choose?" The organist too, immediately began playing the familiar strains of Raymond's favorite, but the chords came to a halt when Raymond moved to the organ and asked her to stop playing.

Raymond approached the pulpit. "Before we join together in song, friends, I'd like to continue in the spirit of Reverend Coons' prayer by sharing some scripture from the Psalm 35." He quickly thumbed through the King James Bible on the pulpit. After briefly glancing down at Daphne, he read: *Plead my cause, O Lord, with them that strive with me: fight against them that fight against me. Take hold of shield and buckler, and stand up for mine help. Draw out also the spear, and stop the way against them that persecute me: say unto my soul, I am thy salvation. Let them be confounded and put to shame that seek after my soul: let them be turned back and brought to confusion that devise my hurt. Let them be as chaff before the wind: and let the angel of the Lord chase them. Let their way be dark and slippery: and let the angel of the Lord persecute them. For without cause have they hid for me their net in a pit, which without cause they have digged for my soul. Let destruction come upon him at unawares; and let his net that he hath hid catch himself: into that very destruction let him fall.*

Raymond paused, looked down at his family and Daphne, and then concluded the scripture reading. *And my soul shall be joyful in the Lord: it shall rejoice in his salvation.*

He stepped back over to the organ and whispered to the organist.

Then he turned back toward the congregation. "Please stand and join me in singing hymn number 127."

Little Frances shrugged her shoulders and flipped through the hymnal as the organ wound up an opening refrain. Daphne immediately recognized the tune. *Onward Christian Soldiers...marching as to-oo war. With the cross of Jee-sus going on before...* As the congregation sang out, Daphne merely mouthed the words. She was tone deaf, and didn't want to ruin what should be a joyful noise. And yet there was something almost *unjoyful* in this song. Something somber. Daphne lifted her eyes from page 127 and stared at Raymond. It was unlike him to take on such a serious tone, yet it echoed the concern she had sensed from him during their drive in his new Ford. His anxiety was unfounded, she thought. Surely the war in Europe was too far away to touch them. In fact, Daphne almost felt that such concern demonstrated a lack of faith in God's protective providence. And she never expected Raymond to be lacking in faith.

Daphne closed her eyes and listened. *Like a mighty a-ar-my moves the church of God; Come, now, we are trea-ding where the saints have trod.* She listened to Raymond's deep baritone, and to Frances too. The sweet, childish soprano came in stark contrast to the hard-edged lyrics: *Gates of hell can never 'gainst that Church prevail...*

As the final sustained note of the song faded, Daphne opened her eyes. The music was replaced by the sound of hymnals returning to the pew racks and worshipers taking their seats. But above the restless rumble, Raymond's voice unexpectedly sang out again: *What a friend we have in Jesus...*

Everyone rose once more.

...All our sins and griefs to bear...

Daphne expected the congregation to immediately join Raymond in his favorite hymn, but for some reason the organist did not play, and the few voices that started to sing along quickly trailed off.

Raymond sang alone.

...O what peace we often forfeit, O what needless pain we bear, All because we do not carry ev'rything to God in prayer.

Daphne turned and looked around the small church. The worshipers stood in silence. Beside her, Frances leaned forward against the dark wood pew. Delmar and Guy Kelley stood stoic and solemn, but Mary and Leona and many others suddenly had the twinkle of tears in their eyes.

As Raymond continued—his rendition slow and soulful, more beautiful than anything she'd ever heard him sing—Daphne felt ashamed for questioning the strength of his faith.

Do thy friends despise, forsake thee? Take it to the Lord in prayer. Raymond's voice grew softer, falling into a warm, melodic whisper. *In His arms He'll take and shield thee. Thou wilt find a solace there.*

The silence that began in the wake of Raymond's solo carried over into the drive to the Abston home. Daphne turned the car radio off and contented herself with sitting next to Raymond, leaning her head against his shoulder.

When they arrived home, the aroma of roast beef, potatoes in rich broth, and homemade noodles had already begun to fill the drafty house. Albert came in from finishing his chores and joined Raymond in the living room while Daphne went into the kitchen to help her mother. But Daphne soon returned and joined the men. "Mother says the roast has another twenty minutes to cook so I should just relax in here with my two favorite men for a while."

When You Come Home

The three of them sat and chatted as the radio played softly in the background. Raymond nodded toward the book on Albert's lap. "What are you reading there?"

Albert picked up the book, carefully displaying the worn cover. "*Book of Poems* by James Whitcomb Riley. He was quite the poet, that man was. Did Daphne mention that years ago Mr. Riley dropped by the old homestead?"

"But that was before I was born, Dad."

"Yes, of course. I guess it was."

Raymond grinned skeptically. "Was this a coulda-been visit like the time maybe-it-was-maybe-it-wasn't-Dillinger who stopped by?"

Albert smiled. "Oh, I'm quite certain it was Mr. Riley. Like Daphne said, it was well before she was born. Could have been before the turn of the century, in fact, when we lived just south of Perry Central School and our road was well traveled by those going north from the middle part of the state. Back then, of course, there were no filling stations or places to get a cold drink, so we were visited frequently by people in dire need of refreshment." He tapped the book. "Oh, it was James Whitcomb Riley all right. Yes sir, he was quite the poet, that man was."

"I'm beginning to think you all should have gotten autographs from everyone who stopped by," Raymond said.

Albert seemingly attempted to deflect the trace of doubt still in the young man's voice. "Speaking of poets, has Daphne recited her little apple tree poem for you yet?"

Daphne laughed. "It was about a cherry tree, not an apple tree, Dad." And besides, it was so silly. I was practically a baby when I wrote it. Of course I haven't shared it with Raymond."

Before Daphne could object, Albert stood and began making broad gestures toward the window as he recited:

Merry little robin
In the cherry tree;
Pick a big ripe cherry
And bring it here to me.

Daphne flushed with embarrassment, but Raymond gave a teasing smile and squeezed her hand. "Maybe it's not quite in Mr. Riley's league, but I think it's sweet."

"Well then, Mr. Kelley, maybe someday I'll write a poem for you. That is, if you treat me right."

"Well, I'll definitely be on my best behavior then, Miss Abston."

"Dinner is almost ready," Maggie announced from the doorway. "By the way, how was the church service this morning?"

"It was nice, Mother. Raymond did a wonderful job leading the congregational singing." Daphne touched his arm. "Your voice is a gift, Raymond."

Raymond's smile was shy. "It's nothing special. I'm sure you sing well too, Daphne."

Daphne didn't miss the amused look that passed between her mother and father.

"But, you know..." Raymond paused as he studied Daphne's face. "I have noticed something."

"Oh? What's that?"

"I can't hear you sing. I guess your voice is so soft the other singers drown it out."

Embarrassed, Daphne spoke quietly. "You can't hear my voice because I'm not singing."

"What did you say?"

Daphne sighed and raised her voice. "Most of the time I just mouth the words. I like to sing, but I can't carry a tune."

Raymond pushed further. "So I guess you wouldn't agree to join me in a duet at church sometime?"

Daphne looked up in time to see her father's eyes twinkle as he chuckled silently behind his hand.

Maggie wiped her hands on her apron and bluntly spoke the truth. "Raymond, you need to understand something. Daphne has a lot of fine qualities, but singing isn't one of them."

A moment of silence hung heavy until Raymond started laughing. Soon they were all chuckling and Daphne decided that not only did Raymond have a fine singing voice, his laugh was rich and pleasing as well.

Later, as they sat down to eat, Albert gave the blessing. The reverend thanked the Lord for the meal, but also asked God's hand on the turmoil and conflict overseas.

As the food was passed, Daphne thought about the morning's worship service and just knew her parents would enjoy hearing Raymond lead the singing at the Milledgeville Methodist Church. "Mother, Dad, would you like to come to Raymond's church with us someday soon?"

"Well I think we would enjoy that, dear," said her mother.

"Perhaps after the first of the year, once Christmas is over," Albert recommended.

Indeed, Christmas was fast approaching, and Daphne knew her parents would like to celebrate the Savior's birth by worshipping in their regular church home.

"That sounds like a great idea," Raymond said, squeezing Daphne's hand beneath the table. "I know my folks would love to meet you, and it'll give us all something to look forward to in the New Year."

After lunch was finished and the dishes cleaned and returned to their shelves, Daphne found Raymond alone in the living room, half asleep, sprawled out in a chair. Lazily, he opened an eye and smiled as he pulled her onto his lap to listen to the radio. It wasn't long before *You are My Sunshine* came over the airwaves. This was her favorite song because, as their courtship had continued, it became *their* song. Softly, Raymond began singing along.

> *The other night dear as I lay sleeping*
> *I dreamed I held you in my arms*
> *When I awoke dear I was mistaken*
> *And I hung my head and cried*
>
> *You are my sunshine my only sunshine*
> *You make me happy when skies are gray*
> *You'll never know dear how much I love you*
> *Please don't take my sunshine away*

With her head against his chest, Daphne could simultaneously hear the richness of his voice and feel the strength of his beating heart.

She felt peaceful. She felt safe—until moments later when she heard the voice of newsman John Charles Daly on the radio:

"The Japanese have attacked Pearl Harbor, Hawaii, by air, President Roosevelt has just announced. The attack also was made on our Naval and Military activities on the principal island of Oahu."

Raymond stood quickly, practically dumping Daphne onto the floor as he ran for the kitchen. Repeating the news story to Maggie, Raymond's words seemed distant and unreal to Daphne. They came out muffled to her ears, the way a voice sounds from beneath the surface of water. After a moment, there came a real silence, and Daphne looked back and forth between Raymond and her mother.

When You Come Home

"Daphne, please go get your father," Maggie said. But before Daphne left the room, she turned back and saw the redness of Raymond's face turn ashen as he said, "I guess we're in the war now, no matter how you look at it."

War. Now it was all too real, too close.

As close as Raymond's heartbeat had been only moments before.

6

Monday, December 8, 1941

ews of the Pearl Harbor devastation grew worse with each radio and newspaper report, with most of the American fleet destroyed in the attack. The battleships Arizona, Utah, Oklahoma, and West Virginia were either sunk or badly damaged. Nineteen other American ships and 188 airplanes were destroyed, with more than 1,100 persons wounded. More than 2,400 were dead.

The attack came as a nightmare surprise. Though folks in the town of Lebanon had been uneasy about the conflicts overseas, their main concern was Adolph Hitler's Nazi takeover of Western Europe. Little attention had been paid to Japan's surging aggression or to faltering U.S./Japanese relations.

In hindsight it seemed the threat should have been recognized. After seizing much of China in the 1930s, Japan shifted its attention to the European colonies in East and Southeast Asia. Because of the empire's invasion into southern Indochina the previous summer, the United States placed an embargo on oil and froze all Japanese assets in the U.S.

When You Come Home

When diplomatic negotiations between the two countries failed, Japan had apparently arranged the sneak attack. Now the whole country was outraged and customers in the Ione Beauty Shop were livid.

It was late in the afternoon while Daphne was lathering Callie Hartman's hair, that a neighboring shopkeeper rushed in with news that President Roosevelt had just addressed the nation by radio. "The United States Congress has declared America in a state of war!" gasped the red-faced man. Feeling a prickly sensation in her spine, Daphne's hands dripped suds as she surveyed the room. The faces looking back at her seemed blank, as if they were uncertain what to do, or even how to respond.

"What in the world?" Mrs. Hartman lifted her soapy head at the announcement and now her bewildered eyes locked with Daphne's. Gently easing the woman's head back down in the basin, Daphne sprayed the remaining soap away and then helped her to an upright position.

Wrapping a white towel around Callie's head, Daphne spoke softly. "I just don't know what to make of all this."

"I'm not at all surprised at the news." Callie Hartman's words became heated. "We can't just let another country attack us unprovoked and not respond."

A few feet away, Mrs. Davidson was bent over her customer ironing the final wave on a "Marcel" hairdo. She straightened up and carefully placed the heavy wooden-handled iron over a small table lamp to keep it warm. Stepping closer to the women, her expression sobered. "You're right about that. So many people killed and injured yesterday . . . and now, God help us, we've entered the war." She shook her head. "Oh Daphne, I sure hope your young man doesn't get called to fight."

Daphne had wrestled with such thoughts, but refused to acknowledge the possibilities. She merely said, "Me too. It took me forever to settle down and fall asleep last night. What about you, Mrs. Davidson?"

Her boss moved back to her booth as she answered the question. "I thought the morning would never come. Most of the night I sat by the radio, afraid I'd miss something, scared that another attack could be coming."

Later, Daphne clipped the last pin curl into place on Mrs. Hartman's fine white hair and walked her to the dryer chair. The older woman turned to her and whispered, "You know, Daphne, I was scared last evening too. In fact, I kept my kerosene lamp going all night."

Daphne gave what she hoped was a reassuring smile, turned the dryer on medium-high, and settled her customer into the chair. She had just returned to her booth to soak her brushes and combs when the front door opened.

"Looks like your next customer is here, dear," noted Mrs. Davidson.

Daphne called a greeting to June Ailes, one of her favorite clients. To Mrs. Davidson she said quietly, "After I get June washed and set, I think I'll head home while it's still daylight, if that's all right with you."

Mrs. Davidson untied the cape around her customer's shoulders and nodded. "Of course. I'm planning to leave real soon myself."

An hour later, as Daphne was sweeping around her work area, she still found herself wavering between righteous indignation, a chilling sense of loss, and the numbness of disbelief. Why, she wondered, hadn't America known far enough in advance to fend off the attack? And what if another strike came or hit closer to home? Heading out to her car, she felt vulnerable and found herself searching the blue skies overhead.

Arriving home, Daphne found her parents sitting at the kitchen table, talking quietly. Albert looked relieved to see his daughter. "Hello Daphne. How was your day?"

She joined her parents at the table. "Well, my feet are killing me, but the rest of me is just numb from the news of the attack, and now I hear we've entered the war. I didn't get a chance to do much more than skim the front page of the paper."

Daphne followed her father's glance. *The Lebanon Reporter* was lying on the corner of the kitchen table. The headlines declared in large bold print: JAPAN MAKES WAR ON U.S. and underneath, in smaller letters: HONOLULU BOMBED, MANY DIE IN SURPRISE ATTACK.

Her father said, "You'll probably want to read the full account of the attack yourself, although the radio accounts are quite similar."

"Folks are pretty frightened right now, aren't they, Dad?"

Albert nodded. "Yes, with good cause. But we can be thankful we live in the middle of the U.S. We've heard that people on the coast are really nervous and may start darkening their windows and shutting out lights at night. Anything to make them less conspicuous from the air, I guess." Her father sighed heavily. "Never thought I'd see the day when Americans were afraid of attack on their own soil."

Maggie spoke up. "I reckon it wouldn't be a bad idea for us to darken our windows at night. What do you think, Albert?"

"Well, I don't think Central Indiana would be a target, but it probably makes sense to take extra precaution for a time."

It saddened Daphne to think of light as a betrayer of safety and security; to know the kind of fear that takes root in darkness. She lifted her head and stared out the kitchen window at the now treacherous sky. "I wonder if Raymond is safely inside right now."

Christmas passed somberly. What should have been a magical time, spending her first Christmas with Raymond, was observed with a strained kind of joy. The season's myriad blessings and messages of hope and peace now seemed fragile.

The winter also seemed unusually long and cold and the promise of spring unthinkable as America was pulled deeper into World War II. Terms like "Allies" and "Axis" began to pepper the conversations of those who followed the battles. Daphne learned that Germany, Italy, and Japan made up the Axis group, with the Allies comprised of Great Britain, France, the Soviet Union, and the United States.

Though the carefree days before December 7 seemed to belong to a different age, the war was still somehow distant, leaving everyone feeling disoriented and displaced. For the time being, though, all they could do was carry on, try to live life as unaffected as possible. And pray for an end to the mushrooming madness.

Somehow life found a new balance. By the time March, 1942 came, birds once again sang of spring, their songs heralding hope as if nothing had changed. But things had changed. There seemed to be an urgency to everything now.

It was a cold, blustery late March wind that followed Mamie Ward into the salon one early afternoon. Daphne was between customers, busy sterilizing hairbrushes and combs. She looked up as the door blew shut. After wiping her hands on a towel, she hurried to greet her friend.

She studied Mamie's eyes. "You look like the cat that swallowed the canary. What's going on?" She touched the girl's short, dark brown locks. This latest style suited Mamie's pretty face. "It's not time for a haircut already, is it?"

A mischievous smile washed over Mamie's face. "No, that's not why I'm here, Daphne. I came in to tell you Jim and I are getting married."

"Oh Mamie, that's wonderful." Daphne hugged her friend. She

truly liked the kind-hearted, gentle farmer Mamie had been dating for quite some time now, and had often wondered just how serious their relationship was becoming. "When's the big day?"

"The 5th of April. It's on a Saturday. We're hoping the weather will warm up a bit by then. And, here's the best news; we want you and Raymond to stand up with us. Jim is going to ask Raymond tonight, so I thought I'd hurry over to ask you first." She took a much-needed deep breath. "So . . . what do you say?"

Daphne was floored. "Well, of course I'll stand up with you. I'd be more than happy to do that. And I'm sure Raymond will be pleased as well." She walked to the window. "My, an April wedding and its already late March. You're certainly going to have a short engagement, aren't you?"

As excited as she was for her friends, Daphne couldn't help being a little envious too, and feeling some sense of urgency. Looking out at a passerby bracing against the headlong wind, she couldn't help wonder: What's keeping Raymond from proposing?

The question just wouldn't go away. All week long Daphne struggled with the temptation to call Raymond. Maybe she should insist he tell her his feelings. But she realized such impulsive behavior could backfire. Besides, her mother's comment stopped her short. "Daphne, nice girls don't call men."

Before Mamie's sudden appearance in the beauty shop, Daphne hadn't thought much about marriage. Now she could think of nothing else. What would it be like to spend the rest of her life as Mrs. Raymond Kelley? As her thoughts moved in that direction, she felt her heart pounding. This man had certainly added excitement to her too-quiet life.

Whenever he whispered charming or funny little endearments in her ear, she found herself giggling like a school girl. And when he held her close and sang along to her father's desktop radio, Daphne melted against him, wishing the song would never end. She suspected she was falling in love with Raymond, but how did he feel about her? If he did care, why in the world hadn't he let her know by now? Surely he wasn't just stringing her along until someone more interesting or appealing came along. Raymond wouldn't do that. Or would he?

7

Saturday, April 5, 1942

I t was a pleasant day—nearing 70 degrees with the sun dancing in and out of fair-weather clouds—for the wedding of Jim Gates and Mamie Ward. Hours earlier, Daphne and Raymond had arrived at the Children's Home parsonage north of town to help with the preparations. Now the photographer was busy snapping pictures of the bride and groom, even though Jim seemed to be wilting in the heat of the bright lights. Raymond found Jim's discomfort highly amusing and taunted him as he dabbed at his friend's face with a towel. "You're going to make Mamie mad if you glow more than she does, pal." Jim smacked at Raymond's hand and grabbed the towel, flicking it toward him with a snap.

Daphne winked at Mamie with a "boys will be boys" look. She rolled her eyes in mock exasperation when Raymond and Jim looked at the two women. "They're sure having a good time, aren't they?" Daphne commented.

Mamie nodded. "My Jim is a soft-spoken man and he's usually quiet until he gets around Raymond. Your guy is good for him." She looked curiously at Daphne. "So how are things going with you two? I can tell you enjoy each other's company."

"Well . . ." Daphne hesitated. "I care a lot for Raymond and I think he feels the same way, but he hasn't told me anything yet."

Mamie shook her head and huffed. "So what's he waiting for?"

"I don't know, but my patience is running out." Daphne's expression was determined. "If he doesn't propose before long, I may just send him on his way."

Mamie looked sideways at Daphne. "Really?"

The giggles attacked Daphne first, then Mamie. Their laughter quickly subsided when Reverend Coons walked over and announced it was now two-thirty and everyone should please come to the front of the room.

Daphne and Raymond took their places next to Jim and Mamie. As the betrothed couple stood quietly before the minister, Daphne stared at her friend. Raymond had been wrong. Jim could never match the glow of his bride.

Daphne looked over and caught Raymond's eyes on her. Smiling slightly, he commanded her gaze. Daphne's heart pounded so fiercely she felt sure the entire congregation could hear it. Gazing at her handsome man across the aisle, she felt the hair on her neck prickle. The almost frightening sensation traveled all the way down to her toes. Suddenly she realized she had forgotten how to breathe. *Heaven help me*, she thought. *I'm in love*.

The next Saturday night, Raymond seemed preoccupied as the couple headed back to the Abston home following a movie. The only light in the empty living room was the kerosene lamp that had been turned down low. Daphne walked over to the marble-topped table and turned the knob of the lamp. The room seemed warm and cozy in the flickering light.

Raymond sat on the sofa and gently pulled Daphne down beside him. It was apparent that something was on his mind.

"Are you all right, Raymond?" Daphne asked.

Raymond looked surprised that she would ask. "I'm okay. But I need to talk with you about something important."

Daphne watched as he stood abruptly and walked over to the photographs on the mantle. Choosing one, he examined it like he'd never seen it before.

"Well, what is it?" Daphne asked, desperately wanting to know.

Raymond put down the frame, crossed the room, and sat down again facing her. He took her hands in his and said, "I've been doing some thinking, honey."

"About what?"

"About you and me. About our future." His eyes held her gaze. "I really look forward to being with you, whether it's going for a drive, catching a movie, or just sitting here on the couch listening to the radio." A flush crept its way into Raymond's face. "When we're apart, I try to invent excuses so I can come by and see you." He cleared his throat and continued. "Do you know what I was thinking while Jim and Mamie were saying their vows?"

Daphne gazed into his eyes as she shook her head.

"I wished it was *us* getting married." He paused for a few seconds to collect himself. "I know I haven't told you this before, but Daphne, I'm in love with you."

Daphne's silence ended. "Oh Raymond, I've been waiting to hear you say those words to me for months." She reached for him and pulled him close, charmed by his startled expression. She laughed and finally cried out, "I love you too!"

Raymond chuckled with Daphne and then pulled away. "I'm glad you love me, but why are you laughing?"

"Because I didn't want to tell you how much I cared about you until I was certain how you felt."

Raymond's face grew serious. "I want you by my side the rest of my life, Daphne." He stopped, took a deep breath and swallowed hard.

"Will you marry me?"

Daphne looked deep into his eyes and then quickly down at their joined hands. When she looked into Raymond's eyes again, she thought she saw sadness there, as if he doubted her response. Only then did she realize she hadn't yet spoken the words that had begun to pulsate with each beat of her heart.

"Oh, Raymond," she whispered, "I'd be honored to be your wife."

8

Saturday, June 20, 1942

fter a nearly sleepless night, Daphne had been up since early morning. *This is my wedding day*, came the refrain in her mind as she hurried around the house helping her mother rearrange furniture, sweep floors, polish glassware, and stack plates and silverware.

As excited as she was, Daphne was also a bit overwhelmed and full of nervous anticipation. In less than three hours family and friends, dressed in their Sunday best, would stroll up to the Abston's front door, eager to witness the most important event thus far in Daphne's life.

But was she ready? Was everything sparkling clean, organized neatly, and in the proper place? Hurrying over to the kitchen table, Daphne shoved aside a stack of newspapers, searching for her slightly crumpled wedding "to do" list. As she scanned the timeline beside each entry, she drew a sigh of relief. She was right on schedule. The only tasks not checked off were the cake and punch, and her mother had ordered her not to worry about the refreshments. Ruth and Bernice would oversee those details.

Daphne guessed that her sisters and their husbands would arrive first, most likely followed by Chester and Mildred. Orville, Jim, and their families lived too far away to make the trip, so Clarence had agreed to set up his camera and capture the memories. Raymond had assured her all of his siblings would be present.

Albert had asked Reverend Carl Metz from the First Baptist Church to officiate the ceremony. A pleasant, middle-aged man, the Reverend had confirmed he would be in place well before two-thirty.

Daphne unexpectedly felt a tinge of sadness as she looked around the home she had shared with her parents. After this day, it would no longer be *hers*. She would become a visitor. From time to time Mrs. Raymond Kelley would come calling on the Abstons.

In the quiet of the house, Daphne sat on the sofa, the same one where Raymond had taken her hands in his and proposed. It had been the first time he confessed his love for her, but he also later confessed his concerns over their future.

"I just don't know what the future holds for us," he told her as the evening wore on. "What with the war going on and . . . well, I'm afraid it's just a matter of time before I receive notice to report for training. What if we get married and I'm sent overseas right away? Oh, Daphne, I just can't bear being apart for months on end."

"I know," Daphne had replied, "but we can't put our lives on hold until after the war. Who knows, maybe the fighting will be over before you're drafted."

That fervent hope had been in her prayers ever since, and even now, in the quiet time before her wedding, Daphne found herself closing her eyes and whispering a plea to God to keep her groom safe and by her side. *To have and to hold. From this day forward.*

When You Come Home

A rap on the door was followed by a chorus of voices entering the living room. Bernice and Ruth, accompanied by their husbands, strode into the house.

Daphne stood quickly, embarrassed at being caught in a brief moment of relaxation on such a busy day. The four visitors stopped in their tracks. No one said a word.

Daphne cocked her head slightly to the side and said, "What is it, Ruth? What's wrong, Bernice?"

Bernice stepped closer to her little sister and her look of concern transformed into one of bemusement. "Honey, what happened to your nose?"

"My nose?"

"It's all red and kind of puffy," said Ruth.

Daphne groaned. She had nearly forgotten about her mishap at the shop the day before. Indeed, when she had gone to bed the night before, the redness had practically disappeared and it had been barely noticeable in the shadows of early morning.

She gasped. "Is it worse?"

"That depends on what it looked like before," Bernice said.

Daphne ran to the hallway mirror and shrieked at the sight. Ruth and Bernice hurried over and Maggie rushed in from outside.

"What is it, Daphne?" Maggie asked.

"It's my nose. Look at it!" Her shoulders slumped as her eyes met the reflected glances of the confused women behind her. "Yesterday, when I was giving a manicure," she explained, "I bent over a little too far and smacked my nose right into the hot bulb of the table lamp." She didn't know whether to laugh or cry as she turned to face her family. "I thought the redness would go away, but it's getting worse. Raymond will take one look at me and run off screaming."

Maggie laughed and touched her daughter's cheek. In the same way she had tried to reassure Daphne about her "snuggies," Maggie repeated, "He probably won't notice, dear. You know how unobservant men can be."

At exactly two-thirty, with her nose camouflaged by expertly blended makeup, Daphne appeared at the entrance to the living room. She was dressed in a long-sleeved, blue and white print chiffon dress and white spectator shoes. A corsage of roses was pinned to her bodice. As her father came forward, he offered his arm and lovingly squeezed her elbow. She looked up and noticed his eyes were moist. "Don't make me cry, Dad," she whispered. "My nose will start glowing again."

The expression on his face softened. "You are glowing all over, dear. You look lovely."

Clutching her father's arm, Daphne walked slowly toward Reverend Metz, who stood in the far corner. Her eyes quickly scanned the packed room. Raymond's family was on her left, and to her right sat her mother, her sisters, and their husbands. A few friends were intermingled as well, including the smiling newlyweds, Jim and Mamie.

The room grew quiet, all eyes on the bride as Daphne neared Raymond, who stood straight and tall at the far end of the room. How handsome her groom looked in his brand new suit. A chill fluttered inside her as her father kissed her on the cheek and released her arm so she could take Raymond's hand in hers. Her heart pounded and she locked her knees in place to keep them from buckling as she practically melted from the tender look on Raymond's face. It was the unmistakable look of love, and surely it was a reflection of the expression on her own face as well.

When You Come Home

Reverend Metz cleared his throat. "Shall we begin?"

Reluctantly, Daphne turned her attention away from Raymond and toward the minister. So lost was she in her happiness that the reverend's words became muted by her euphoria. But suddenly she felt Raymond slipping the small gold band with the heart-shaped diamond onto her finger. She heard a voice that sounded something like her own saying, "I do," and a voice that sounded vaguely like Raymond's saying the same. Within her dizzying emotions she heard "man and wife," and then felt Raymond's lips against hers.

"Dear friends, I'd like to present to you, Mr. and Mrs. Raymond Kelley."

The once quiet room erupted into joyous applause as everyone crowded around the couple, shaking hands, patting backs, and offering congratulations. Afterwards, the guests trailed behind Daphne and Raymond into the kitchen.

"Here Raymond, you get the very first piece of wedding cake," Bernice announced as she slipped a large piece of her homemade German Chocolate cake onto a plate. "And, Daphne, how about you? I know you weren't hungry earlier, with all the bustling around and all."

"Well, I'm certainly hungry now that things have settled down," Daphne said. She accepted a slice and took a large bite. "Oh, Bernice, this is absolutely luscious," she said before swallowing, her words a bit muffled. A moment later she added, "And, Ruth, the punch looks so pretty. You got it just the right shade of rose, exactly like I asked for."

Ruth grinned and handed Daphne a cup. She gave one to Raymond, who downed it before Daphne could take her first sip. Raymond tugged at his stiff shirt collar. "It's got to be over 90 degrees outside. I can't imagine what the temperature is here in the house. This suit is just downright hot, ladies."

Jim and Mamie walked into the kitchen in time to hear Raymond's remark. Jim snickered. "Well, I guess being hot under the collar on your wedding day is better than getting cold feet."

Raymond laughed and as soon as he placed his empty cup on the table, Jack Abston handed him a fresh one. "Well, my good man," Jack said, "this is another reason for me to hold off getting married for a long, long time. It wouldn't be proper for me to lose my cool in front of the whole family." He eyed Daphne. "Huh, Daphna?"

Everyone laughed but Raymond. He was looking into Daphne's eyes, his expression sweet and tender. Daphne felt her heart flutter again and as she put down her glass of punch, Raymond reached for her hand. "This is the best day of my life, sweetheart," he whispered, "and you look absolutely gorgeous."

Daphne looked up at him. She had never considered herself even pretty, let alone gorgeous, but at that moment, seeing the love and truth in her husband's eyes, she *felt* quite beautiful, red nose and all.

A half hour later the noisy group gathered outdoors for family photos in the hot sunshine and strong wind. Daphne struggled to hold her dress down in the swirling breeze with one hand while hanging onto her handsome husband with the other.

Soon afterward, the newlyweds were on the road in Raymond's car, tin cans clattering along behind. As Daphne snuggled up next to her new husband, they set off for northern Indiana to enjoy a short honeymoon. Once they were out of town, Raymond stopped the car and tenderly kissed his bride. He stepped out of the car and untied the cans from the bumper. "Too noisy," he said, "and I don't want one flying through someone's windshield and hurting them." As usual, Raymond was thinking more of others than of himself. It was one of the positive qualities Daphne loved about this dear man.

Back on the road again, Daphne barely noticed the scenery racing past her car window. She was thinking about her life with Raymond, about how wonderful it was going to be, about all the places they would see together, all they would do. She was thinking about the children they would raise. But she was also thinking that it would all have to wait. Still, at that moment they were alone in the whole universe, just the two of them, arm-in-arm and heart-to-heart. And it was perfect.

"Do you remember the night I proposed?"

Daphne's daydreaming surrendered to Raymond's question. She laughed with an unexpected and unladylike snort as she said, "How could I forget? I thought you'd never ask me to marry you. In fact, I had told Mamie a week or two earlier that I was about ready to send you on your way if you didn't propose pretty soon."

Raymond turned to her. "Oh, honey, don't say that. It scares me to think I might have lost you." He continued to look at her for a moment, his face softening as he looked back toward the road. "I was so excited the night you agreed to marry me, I laughed and sang all the way back to Indianapolis. I'm sure anyone passing me on the road thought I was a lunatic."

Daphne laughed. "Maybe they just knew you were in love," she said. Raymond gently kissed her hand and she nuzzled deeper against him.

When Lebanon was hours behind them with the sun dipping lower in the cloudless sky, Raymond suggested they find a room. A few minutes later, on the southern side of South Bend, Indiana, he guided the Ford into the parking lot of a small hotel. After registering at the front desk, the newlyweds were handed a set of keys and directed to their room.

When they reached the room, they both stopped and stared at the door. Raymond looked over at his young bride with raised eyebrows as if to say, *Okay, dear, this is it.* Daphne smiled to cover her apprehension, but suspected it was only natural for them both to be nervous. Beyond that door was the beginning of their life together.

As the sun set and darkness befell the sky, Daphne and Raymond settled into the room and into each other's loving embrace. The night became theirs and hardly a moment passed when they were not in each other's arms, delighting in a closeness they had only dared to imagine before.

The next morning, still clinging to one another and dreading their return to the outside world, they nonetheless made plans to seek out Raymond's aunt Mae, who lived in South Bend. Daphne had laughed when Raymond told her his aunt's name was "Mae West." When they arrived at the Vining home, Daphne was happy to meet her new relatives, but a bit disappointed that this Mae West was nothing like the buxom blonde bombshell from the movies.

They spent the entire day with Mae and the Vinings, and the following morning all headed north to the beach in Benton Harbor on Lake Michigan. Reveling beneath the warm sun, Daphne tried to keep her still tender nose from becoming sunburned as they shared a picnic lunch on the sand. They all returned to South Bend later that night, happy and exhausted.

The next morning the honeymooners headed home and rolled into Lebanon late Monday afternoon. After stopping at their new second-story apartment to freshen up, they drove out to the Abston home.

Around eight o'clock that night, several young people, including Jim and Mamie, neighbors and church friends, showed up unexpectedly at the Abston farmhouse. Albert and Maggie were out back sitting in the shade, leaving Raymond to answer the door. Daphne watched a suspicious look wash over his face as he invited the noisy group into the living room.

Daphne stepped forward as the group surrounded her and Raymond. Her nose, now blistered, drew the attention of Louis Riddle, one of Raymond's close friends. Frowning, he strode heavily across the room and stared at her face. "Has Raymond been smacking you in the nose, Daphne? Or have you been crying or something?"

"Maybe she fell asleep in the sun," someone else said.

Mamie shoved her way through the crowd. "Oh come on, you guys. Quit making such a fuss." She examined Daphne's nose. "Well, let's see. A few blisters, but the redness seems to have softened somewhat, wouldn't you say, Daph?"

"Oh, it's nothing compared to how it looked a few days ago. And Raymond doesn't seem to mind, do you dear?"

Raymond smiled a smile that Daphne felt was meant only for her. "It just adds a little more glow to your lovely face," he said. He bent down and kissed the tip of her nose.

Exaggerated throat-clearing interrupted the tender moment and someone yelled, "We'd better get going before these newlyweds get all lovey-dovey on us."

Raymond's eyebrows rose. "You're leaving already?"

Jim edged his way between his newly-married friends. Working hard to be serious, he said, "Well, actually, you're both coming with us into town. And you'll ride with Mamie and me." He turned to the others and raised his voice. "All right, folks. We'll meet you at the north side of the courthouse. Let's head out!"

Raymond was smiling now. He bent his head down and whispered to Daphne, "I have a feeling they're going to shivaree us around town, my dear."

Daphne laughed. "Sure looks that way."

Whooping like crazed warriors, the young people crammed into three cars, drove to town and pulled up outside the new jail across from the courthouse. With much fanfare, they all bounded out of the cars to assist in loading Daphne into a wheelbarrow. The group goaded Raymond into wheeling his young bride, her legs up in the air, around the downtown square. Their boisterous friends paraded along behind and townspeople pointed and laughed as the caravan traveled by.

Next, in keeping with tradition, the bride and groom were locked in a Boone County jail cell for nearly twenty minutes. The Kelleys played right along and, after much laughter, shouting, and teasing, were released. When the rituals subsided and everyone finally settled down, the group headed back to the Abston farm to watch the newlyweds open their wedding gifts.

After the last guest departed, Raymond helped Daphne load the gifts, the rest of her clothes, and a few other belongings into the car before heading to their apartment on the east side of town. Their newly rented home was furnished, though the furniture was sparse and plain. And though Daphne looked forward to the day she could select furniture for a permanent residence, for now this little space would do just fine.

For wherever Raymond was, so was her heart.

And her heart had found a home.

9

Summer, 1942

Daphne thrived in her role as Mrs. Raymond Kelley. In her new husband she had found a friend, a shoulder to lean on, and someone to share her life with, no matter what. Her sense of fulfillment deepened as her feelings for the man she married grew with each passing day.

Though she continued to work at the Ione six days a week, Daphne arranged her schedule to leave plenty of time at each day's end to spend with Raymond. His eight-to-five job usually allowed him to arrive home before Daphne, and when she would finally reach their tiny apartment, seeing his eyes light up erased the worries of the day. Even the weariness in her feet from standing all day seemed insignificant.

Still a novice at preparing meals, the young bride enjoyed honing her culinary skills while learning the foods Raymond liked most.

"What's for supper tonight, sweetheart?" Raymond slipped up behind his wife, gently massaging the back of her neck. Daphne turned from the oven, hot pad in hand.

"Another new recipe," she announced.

Raymond responded guardedly. "Oh, boy . . ."

"Now Raymond, most of my creations have been fairly tasty." Daphne dared him to disagree. "Haven't they?"

Raymond chuckled. "For the most part. But what's in the oven *now*?"

Daphne cupped her empty hand into a pretend microphone and altered her voice. "This evening's feature is a casserole the new Mrs. Kelley discovered last week in her *Good Housekeeping* magazine." She gave her husband a little pat and turned her attention back to the stove. "Now, Mr. Kelley, will you please move aside."

"Yes ma'am."

Daphne opened the oven and carefully lifted out the bubbling dish. Raymond peered over her shoulder. "Mmmm. Looks good and smells good. What's *in* it?"

"New potatoes, peas, carrots, white sauce, and left-over shredded pork roast. I put baking powder biscuits on the top."

Soon they were seated at the table. Raymond reached over and took Daphne's hand. Daphne loved to hear her husband pray. "Dear Heavenly Father, thank you for this food that Daphne has prepared and thank you for meeting our daily needs. Please watch over us, guide us, and keep us ever mindful of your Word. In Jesus' name, Amen."

As they ate, Raymond asked Daphne about her day, and she shared an incident concerning a difficult customer. "Junelle Simmons dropped off her sister, Sarah Beth, for a haircut and set. As I worked on her hair, we chatted. She told me she lived in Clinton, Indiana. She wasn't much of a talker, but she seemed nice enough. That is, until I finished. I couldn't believe it. She put on her glasses, took a long look at herself in the mirror, and frowned. It was evident she didn't like my work. I was surprised because I thought the style suited her face nicely."

"Maybe her glasses needed an adjustment," Raymond commented in a serious tone. The corners of his mouth moved ever so slightly, and his chest began to shake as he stifled a laugh.

Daphne eyed him sternly. "Raymond, don't you dare. I began reshaping her hair on the sides and fluffing up her bangs. Finally, she seemed satisfied."

Raymond smiled. "So all was well?"

"No, not entirely. When she was ready to leave, I told her the total cost was one dollar and twenty-five cents. She looked at me with surprise and said, 'It's how much?' I repeated the amount and she said, 'Well, where I get my hair done regularly, it's a lot less than that for a cut and set.'"

"I just stood there and stared at her. After all the time and attention I gave her, I couldn't believe she was bickering about the price. I really had to hold my tongue to keep from saying, 'Well, we're *not* in Clinton now, are we?'"

Raymond snickered.

"But I smiled somehow and said, 'I'm sorry, but that's pretty much the price most salons charge here in Lebanon.' Lucky for both of us, her sister pulled up in the alley next to the shop right then. She laid down the exact change and stomped out. So . . . how was *your* day, honey?"

"A bit out of the ordinary. This morning my supervisor mentioned that a Jewish rabbi had arrived to bless meat. I wanted to know more about it, so I looked through the door glass into the slaughtering room. For several minutes, I watched the rabbi carefully examine the organs and various cuts, then pray over them, so they could be considered kosher. It was hard to tear myself away, but I had to go back to work."

"How often does the rabbi come?"

Raymond shook his head. "I don't know. This was the first time I've ever seen him." Raymond took a sip of water. "Then after lunch, I spent a couple of hours training our new employee on operating the grinder. Gerald seems to be a rather solemn fellow, but very quick to pick up on the little details of the job. I think he'll work out fine."

"Is he married?"

"Yes. In fact, his wife just had twin baby girls last week."

"Really?" Daphne laid down her fork. "Oh, Raymond, wouldn't it be fun to have twin babies some day?"

"Twin girls?"

"I was thinking more like twin boys. But it'd be nice to have a girl or two as well."

Raymond wiggled his eyebrows. "Guess we'd better get started then."

Daphne aimed a playful punch at her husband's arm. "About your coworker, where does he live?"

"South of Indianapolis, but his wife's family lives in Boone County. In fact, they own a farm just a few miles south of your folks. Which reminds me, sometime soon we need to drive out to your parents' house to check our mail."

Daphne nodded thoughtfully. It seemed strange not to receive any letters or bills at the apartment, but Raymond had arranged with the Lebanon post office to deliver their mail to the Abston residence. He considered the apartment to be a temporary residence for both of them until the war forced them to make other plans.

"Why don't we drive out to see Mother and Dad after supper?" Daphne asked as she took a forkful of the flakey casserole crust.

"Good idea. Then we can circle around and visit with my family too."

When You Come Home

When they finished eating, Daphne got up from the table and carried the dirty plates and half-empty casserole dish into the kitchen. Reaching toward the back of the countertop, she lifted a glass cake cover and carefully slid out the applesauce cake she had baked on Sunday evening while Raymond was away from the apartment.

After carving out two generous slices of cake, Daphne carried the little plates to the table. "I made your favorite, applesauce cake."

Raymond looked hopeful. "Did you use my mother's recipe?"

Daphne smiled. "Yes. I followed it word-for-word. So, go ahead, try it." She studied Raymond's face as he took a bite and closed his eyes. "Well, what do you think?"

Raymond opened one eye, then the other. He sighed. "Well, Daphne, it's um, it's..." Daphne could feel her shoulders sag. She looked down at her lap. And then Raymond began laughing. "Oh, honey, it's perfect. I knew there was a reason I married you."

Daphne exhaled loudly, giggled, and dug into her piece of cake. She made a mental note to give Leona a call later on and thank her for sharing the recipe. "By the way, Mamie stopped by the beauty shop today. She wondered if we'd like to meet her and Jim at the Avon this Saturday night for a movie."

"How are we doing with our money? Can we afford a date?"

Daphne did some fast calculations in her head. "Let's see, the movie will cost thirty-five cents apiece, and if we buy popcorn, that will be a dime. And two bottles of Coke will cost two more nickels."

"So we're going to spend close to a dollar on our date night."

Daphne nodded. "We both get paid this Friday and our rent isn't due for another two weeks, so we should be able to manage just fine. I'll call Mamie tomorrow from work and finalize the plans. I wonder what's playing that night."

"I'll look," Raymond said. "Where's tonight's paper?"

"Somewhere in the kitchen," replied Daphne. "Tell you what. I'll bring you the paper if you'll rub my feet."

Raymond grinned. "It's a deal."

Daphne retrieved *The Lebanon Reporter* from the kitchen counter and handed it to her husband. She propped her feet on his lap and sighed with pleasure as he gently massaged away the aches of the day.

Raymond skimmed the headlines and grimaced. "The news from overseas just gets worse and worse. How can Hitler continue to be so powerful? He's taking control over one country after another." He sighed. "I don't think we're going to see an end to the fighting any time soon."

"I heard that Frank McDonald signed up last week," Daphne said quietly, hoping to measure Raymond's reaction to the news.

Raymond looked up. "Don't worry, honey. I'm not going to change my mind about enlisting. I'll fight if and when I'm called, but I'm not going to leave you until I have to."

Daphne forced herself to set aside thoughts about the war. Her life was too enjoyable to allow what was happening thousands of miles away to trouble her as deeply as it affected so many others. At times she felt guilty for her bliss. She even tried to keep her happiness in check so others wouldn't think her naïve or foolish or unpatriotic.

But she was none of those things. She was in love. More deeply than ever. And that made the world a wonderful place.

All too quickly the hot caress of summer drew to an end, and the refreshingly mild days of September disappeared as well. Soon the leaves on the trees along the Abston's long driveway became richly hued in the colors of autumn. Daphne loved this time of year when the foliage turned to luscious reds, oranges, and yellows even as a hint of winter began to color the air.

On a clear Sunday afternoon in October, Daphne gazed up adoringly at her young husband. Despite the cool breeze, the sun felt warm on her shoulders as they strolled, hand-in-hand toward the farmhouse for a visit with her folks.

Totally absorbed in each other, the young lovers didn't notice Maggie watching them from the kitchen window. A solemn-looking Albert met them at the door and hurried them inside. Before they could sit down, Maggie pulled a long envelope from her apron pocket and handed it to Raymond. He sat down on the kitchen chair and tore open the ominous letter. As he began silently reading, his face grew serious. Daphne was instantly concerned and stepped closer to look over his shoulder. The capital letters at the top of the paper immediately caught her eye: "ORDER TO REPORT FOR INDUCTION." Raymond's full name and induction number were typed several spaces below the heading.

As Daphne absorbed the grim contents of the document, Raymond spoke in a voice that was now quiet and somber. "I'm to report to the local Selective Service Board to determine my eligibility for training and service in the Army."

Daphne stopped reading and looked into her husband's face. His eyes pleaded for reassurance, but she didn't know how to make this nightmare go away.

Albert put a hand on his son-in-law's shoulder. "When are you leaving?"

Raymond held Daphne's gaze for a moment longer before responding. "It says I'm to meet with the local board at the Lebanon Armory on October 26. From there, it will be determined when and where I'll report for training."

Suddenly it seemed to Daphne as if a black cloud had blotted out the sun. Her idyllic little slice of the universe was being threatened and she was powerless to defend it.

10

Sunday, November 8, 1942

" Happy Anniversary, Mother and Dad," Daphne said as she hugged her beaming parents. In the midst of the family's celebration of Maggie and Albert's 45th wedding anniversary, Daphne tried to keep her mood light and festive. Nonetheless, she felt a strong sense of disquiet, almost panic, in fact. Raymond was to report for basic training the next day, and she couldn't fathom being away from him for days on end, let alone months or years.

Two weeks earlier, Raymond had met with the local Army board and been ordered to report for assignment to Fort Benjamin Harrison on Monday, November 9. Since then, Daphne had done her best to put it out of her mind, but his departure had become painfully real just hours earlier when they packed their precious, but few, belongings and moved out of the furnished apartment.

After their few months of togetherness, they had come full circle. She and Raymond would be apart, and Daphne would return to her bedroom in the Abston home. Even though she had been gone only a short time, the house suddenly seemed like merely that—a house—not a home. Not *her* home anyway. Not anymore. Though she knew her parents would enjoy having her back and would do their best to make everything seem like old times, Daphne was struck by the realization that things would never be the same.

Her home was with Raymond. Soon that would only be a place in her heart.

Daphne left the family gathering for a moment, making her way from the kitchen to the too-small bedroom she would occupy again. On the bed were two bulging suitcases. She would empty hers later in the day, but Raymond's would remain packed for his extended time away from home. She had helped him gather up his clothes and personal items, and managed to smile as he showed her the pictures and other small mementos he would keep in his wallet. She had even successfully fended off the tears, though they nearly came when Raymond showed her the lock of her own red hair that he vowed to keep with him.

Now, as she stared at the bags on the bed, the tears were again close to the surface.

"You should be with the rest of the family," Raymond said as he came up behind her and took her shoulders in his broad hands. He leaned down and kissed the top of her head. "I'll see to it that there's time for us later tonight, sweetheart."

Daphne waited until she was certain the tears in her eyes would not fall. Then bravely she turned and smiled at her husband. Leaning into his chest, she held him tight. "Oh Raymond, today we're celebrating my parent's anniversary. We'll talk, laugh, eat cake, and pretend everything is fine. But it's *not* fine. Tomorrow, I'll watch you board a train and you'll be gone for weeks, months, or years." Daphne choked back a sob. "Why couldn't you have flunked your stupid physical?"

Raymond grinned and held her closer. "Because I'm no 4-F. It'll be all right, Mrs. Kelley. Many other couples have gone through this. Surely we can do it too."

Daphne shut her eyes and whispered the one thought that had haunted her since Raymond received his induction papers: "But what if something happens to you and you don't come back?"

Raymond tightened his arms around her. "Don't even think such a thing. I'll be back. I've got too much waiting for me here. And so many things I want to do when I come back."

Daphne's voice was so soft Raymond had to bend his head to hear. "Like going back to school and training for the ministry?"

Raymond nodded. "I fully intend to make you a preacher's wife someday." He attempted some humor. "That's probably a step up from being "the preacher's daughter."

Daphne had to laugh, though her eyes filled with fresh tears. "You always know how to make me feel better."

Raymond gave his wife a long, tender kiss and released her. "We'd better get back to the others before they wonder where we are."

Together, they walked down the hall to the kitchen.

There, family members crowded around the table, reminiscing while they nibbled on anniversary cake. Inevitably, the talk always turned to the war. Soon everyone but Daphne was drawn into the conversation. She desperately wanted to get away and leave such talk behind. She felt sick when Jack announced he had been called for duty and assigned to the Signal Corps. Her nephew's usual cockiness was missing, replaced with a trace of uncertainty as he shared news of his soon-to-be overseas deployment.

A pall of quiet overcame the group.

Finally, Ruth said, "Enough talk of war. I hear you've got a new typewriter, Daphne. Let's test it, shall we?"

Daphne got to her feet and led the way into the parlor. There on a flimsy end table sat the shiny new Remington, a stack of paper beside it. Bernice pulled a chair up to the machine and rolled a piece of paper into it. With fast keystrokes, she typed, *Raymond, you are a bad boy.*

Over the group's laughter, Raymond said, "Okay ladies, step aside. It's my turn now." He sat down, looked up at Daphne, then painstakingly pecked out, *I Love You Sweetheart.* Reading over his shoulder, Daphne laughed, though again she felt the tears welling up. Raymond must have seen her expression because his face softened as he continued typing: *Dear Daphne, let not your heart be troubled. Ye believe in God, believe also in me. Love Raymond.*

When he looked up at her again, Daphne saw in his eyes a love far more permanent and encouraging than the typewritten words. But even so, she pulled the paper from the Remington, folded it a couple of times and tucked it into her dress pocket. Just as Raymond would keep mementos of her while he was away, she decided to keep mementos of him. They would be memories she could hold in her hands, just as she would hold Raymond in her heart until he could come back home.

When You Come Home

11

Monday, November 9, 1942

Early the next morning, with the day promising to be unseasonably warm, the Big Four Depot on the west side of Lebanon bustled with wives, sweethearts, mothers, and fathers gathered to see off their servicemen. Some thirty men were bound for Fort Benjamin Harrison in Indianapolis to await their assignments. Raymond wasn't the only Kelley to be heading out. His brother Floyd had been ordered to report as well, and he and his wife Twyla arrived at the train station shortly after Daphne and Raymond. Twyla, seven months pregnant with the couple's first child, clung to her husband and cried uncontrollably.

Daphne looked away, only to discover a crowd of sad strangers, most of them in tears. So many despairing and distraught souls. There were brave faces too, including Raymond's. He was working hard to keep smiling as he talked with his mother.

As the time to leave grew near, Raymond took Daphne in his arms. Feeling the emotion rise up as she clung to him, Daphne concentrated on her breathing. Sucking in her husband's clean, masculine scent, she was determined to capture and hold its very essence until they were together again. When the threat of tears waned, she pulled back and looked up into his blue eyes. "Honey, what was your mother saying to you?"

Raymond forced a smile and swallowed hard. "She just said, 'Raymond, they might take your life, but they can't take your soul.'"

Daphne said only, "Oh," certain that more words would bring a torrent of tears. She hugged Raymond tightly until at last she managed to whisper, "I love you, and I'll write every day."

"I love you too, sweetheart," he said, his words full of emotion as he released her and started toward the train. "I promise to write back." He blew her a kiss as he waited to board, and Daphne reached up into the air and caught it as if the kiss had weight and form.

Guy and Leona Kelley stood off to the side, looking on somberly as their boys boarded the train. As sad as she was for herself, Daphne ached as much for her in-laws, knowing how heavy their hearts must be at parting with *two* of their sons on the same day. Standing quietly beside the older couple as the train pulled away, she furiously blinked back tears. She would be strong. She *would not* cry.

Her parents met her at the door. Their faces were full of compassion, but they merely smiled and allowed her to go to her room, apparently knowing that all she needed at that moment was solitude. But as Daphne crossed the floor and sat on the bed, the quiet, the loneliness, and the *loss* hit her full force.

She ran to her father and collapsed on his lap, sobbing.

"There, there," he said a couple of times, but that was all he could say. He just held his little redheaded girl, patting her back and stroking her hair tenderly for the longest time, until her tears were spent.

When You Come Home

It was dark outside and Daphne still hadn't finished settling into her old bedroom. With great effort she shoved her suitcase across the room and threw it on the bed. Then, woodenly, she began the task of transferring clothing, shoes, toiletries, and keepsakes from bed to dresser to closet.

"Hello Daphne."

Daphne looked up. "Bernice! When did you get here?"

"A few minutes ago." Her older sister tried to smile as she leaned against the door jam. "You were making so much noise hauling your suitcases around the room that you didn't hear me come in the front door. Mother's in bed, so Dad let me in."

"Are you spending the night?"

"No. I have to be back in Indianapolis to teach tomorrow. I just dropped by to check on you. How are you doing, honey?"

Daphne perched on the edge of the bed and sighed. "This is so much harder than I thought it would be. I feel hollow and empty inside."

Bernice's face softened and she walked over and sat next to her sister. Giving Daphne a gentle hug, she said, "It will get easier. I just hope it won't be long until this horrible war ends and Raymond is home."

"Me too."

Bernice looked with interest at the object in Daphne's hand. "What's that?"

Daphne held up the square piece of cardboard emblazoned with a large blue star about six inches wide. "These stars have been produced especially for the war. The president wants every family with a member in the service to buy a star and display it in a window as an act of patriotism and support."

Bernice's interest was piqued. "I read about the stars in the paper just the other day. Aren't there several colors?"

"Yes." Daphne continued, "Blue for the family of a person stationed in the States, silver for those who have someone fighting overseas, and gold in memory of a loved one killed in the service.

"Well, it's a nice way to honor our soldiers," Bernice said. "Let's see how it looks in your window."

Together the women taped the shiny blue star to the bedroom window, presenting it to the pitch-dark night.

The war was now very personal to Daphne. She looked at Bernice and her voice faltered. "I wonder if they're all as scared as I am."

Bernice had no magic words to dispel her sister's anguish. After brushing Daphne's cheek with a kiss, she said quietly, "I'd better let you finish putting things away."

Daphne nodded, but didn't get up. Instead, she sighed heavily. After Bernice left the room, Daphne hugged her pillow to her chest. "Star light, star bright," she began, but then the tears came once more and she fell upon her bed, crying and feeling the full weight of exhaustion. Her emotional fatigue told her the stars in the sky could no longer grant wishes, for they were too busy keeping watch over fields of war.

Prayers. Yes, prayers were infinitely more powerful, because God Himself was the keeper of those wishes. But as Daphne lay sobbing on her bed, all she could manage to pray was "Oh Lord, please . . ." And then, in her weariness, she was certain she could hear Raymond singing, *In His arms He'll take and shield thee. Thou wilt find a solace there.*

12

Sunday, November 29, 1942

*D*o you know you are my sunshine?

A voice. An echo. Raymond.

Daphne squinted and sat up in bed. She searched the darkness for her husband, but there was only...smoke! She tried to cry out, tried to scramble from beneath the covers.

It's all right, sweetheart, it's all right, don't be afraid.

Raymond's voice calmed her and she realized it wasn't smoke at all. It was only steam, steam from her breath. But why was there so much steam and why had her room turned so cold?

The walls disappeared and from nowhere Daphne heard a train whistle. Then she saw Raymond. Saw him in the haze. Saw his smile and his bright blue eyes breaking through the colorless night.

He started to reach out for her, but suddenly withdrew his hand. Instead, he reached up into the night sky and pulled something from the mist.

It's blue, he said, holding up the cardboard star for her to see. It means I'm gone, but not so very far away, really.

Daphne reached for her husband, but as he came toward her the fog closed in and her hand disappeared into the void where Raymond's smile had been. Quick tears came to her eyes, and as she blinked, the tears erased the mist and painted in its place the dark walls of her bedroom.

She pulled her fingers back toward her own face and touched her cheek. *Why could these fingers feel the skin of her own body, yet feel nothing of Raymond's presence?* But as her open eyes adjusted to the nighttime, she knew. She could feel nothing of Raymond because there was nothing to feel. He had been only a dream, and dreams had no substance.

They were made of longings.

13

Wednesday, December 18, 1942

Daphne opened a dresser drawer and removed several pairs of socks and piled them on top of the dresser. When she closed the drawer, the candy necklace Raymond had given her for her birthday the previous year clacked against the wood of the drawer beneath. She smiled and turned toward the oval mirror on the wall. The tiny movie ticket birthday card was wedged into the space between the glass and the wood frame. Turning back to the dresser, she opened another drawer and removed from it some undergarments, including her pink snuggies.

As she prepared for her trip to Hattiesburg, Mississippi, reminders of Raymond were everywhere. Reassuring as they were, however, Daphne did not need them to keep Raymond in her thoughts. He was inside her head all the time. And though his presence in her life was a godsend, his absence made each day a lifetime in itself. The past few days had been no different in that regard, though now the days were long not because of her despair at their separation, but rather from her anticipation of their planned reunion.

While visiting with Raymond's mother Leona and his sister Mary, Daphne made the decision to go see Raymond for Christmas. Though the women tried to cheer Daphne, it soon became clear the only cure for her melancholy would be joining Raymond at Camp Shelby in Hattiesburg where his unit, Company C of the Army's 85th Division, was in basic training. "Maybe I *should* go visit Raymond," Daphne said as the women chatted over coffee. "I've already discussed taking time off from the shop with Mrs. Davidson."

"Well it would certainly be better than being miserable for Christmas, dear," Leona said. "But do you have enough money to make the trip?"

"I will if the Army forwards Raymond's check in time."

"I have some money saved, Daphne," Mary said. "And I'll be glad to loan it to you."

Daphne was touched by Mary's generosity, especially considering how tight finances were in the Kelley household, but they all agreed to wait a couple of days to see if Raymond's allotment showed up.

Raymond's commission check for twenty-one dollars arrived the next day and Daphne made arrangements to visit her husband. The days since had seemed just as long as those before, but now they were happy, expectant days.

As Daphne and her parents made their way to the Greyhound Bus Station at the corner of South and Meridian Streets in downtown Lebanon, they passed the Ione Beauty Shop. Daphne pecked on the cold window as she passed, and when Ione Davidson looked up, Daphne lifted up the bus ticket she had purchased a few days earlier. The older woman nodded and gave a little wave, reminding Daphne of the sacrifice Mrs.

Davidson was making by allowing her to take time off. Though Daphne had promised to make up the time by working extra hours between trips, Mrs. Davidson at first had said, "I'm not sure it's the right thing for you to be gallivanting all over the USA just to steal a few days with your husband." Nonetheless, she quickly relented. "But I suppose common sense never did win out over love. So I guess we'll just all pull together to make sure your customers are taken care of."

Maggie called to her daughter. "Hurry up, honey, or you'll miss your bus."

"I'm coming, Mother."

Daphne waved a gloved hand to the other beauticians who would also cover for her while she was gone. She ran to catch up with her parents.

When they reached the station, Bonnie Stout was waiting for them. Bonnie was heading to Mississippi to visit her brother Jim who was also at Camp Shelby. Daphne knew the attractive blonde because of Jim's wife May, who waitressed at Fleming's Lunch. Daphne and May had become friends one lunch at a time, and during a few of those lunches, Daphne had gotten to know Bonnie as well.

"Now you be sure to give Raymond our love, dear."

"Oh, I will, Mother. Bye, Dad." Daphne hugged both her parents. "I'll call you when I get there."

The bus ride was as she expected—long and uncomfortable. The bus was freezing and there was little room to stretch out, even for one as petite as Daphne. She and Bonnie grew fidgety and looked forward to each of the Greyhound's infrequent stops.

The stop at Memphis, Tennessee included a change of buses and while they waited in the cool night air to board their new coach, two drunken young men slowly circled them. The men nudged each other until the taller of the two, speaking in a thick drawl, slurred, "Hey, little la-a-a-a-dies, where y'all goin?'"

Daphne and Bonnie averted their eyes and Daphne tried to hold her breath to avoid inhaling the stench of whiskey fouling the air.

"Whatsa matter, purty lil thangs . . . cat got yer lips?"

At that the short one standing before Daphne howled with laughter. "Cat lips!" he roared, spittle running down his unshaven chin.

Bonnie rolled her eyes, but Daphne felt like her heart was going to jump out of her chest.

Tall-drunk took a menacing step closer to Bonnie. "You must be one of them yeller cats," he said, daring to stroke her new fur-lined coat and then reaching for her blonde hair. Bonnie recoiled from his touch as the other one said to Daphne, "So what kinda purty little kitty has red hair?"

Anger and disgust replaced Daphne's fear. She took a step toward him, pointing at her tormentor bravely. "Get out of here!"

Tall-drunk roared with laughter and fended off the jabs of his buddy.

The girls hurriedly boarded the frigid bus for the final leg of their journey. Once seated, Bonnie squeezed Daphne's arm. "You really stood up to those drunks, Daphne. Weren't you scared?"

"Well . . . not at that moment. I was too offended." But now Daphne felt her body begin to tremble with delayed reaction to the frightful episode. She closed her eyes in relief and murmured a prayer for God's continued protection.

The women were dozing when the bus approached downtown Hattiesburg. As the Greyhound hissed to a stop beneath the bright lights of the station, Daphne opened her eyes and jostled Bonnie awake.

When You Come Home

Straightening her clothes and fluffing her hair, Daphne peered out the window hoping to spot Raymond. But the glare made it difficult to see the faces of those waiting for the bus to unload.

As she anxiously waited for the passengers in the rows ahead of her to disembark, Daphne finally reached the steps and heard Raymond's deep voice calling her name. Her tired eyes scanned the gathering until she spotted her husband. He was dressed in a drab green uniform and sported a new army haircut. He waved his arms wildly and pushed his way through the crowd.

"Raymond!" Daphne yelled, blowing him a kiss as she stepped off the bus. Playfully, Raymond reached down toward the ground as he continued to run, pretending to scoop up the kiss.

Then, together at last, Raymond picked up his bride and kissed her. She tasted his lips and the scent of him overpowered her. He spun her around until she was dizzy. Maybe it was only the spinning that made her that way. Or maybe it was the lights and the bus fumes, or perhaps her own weariness.

But as she squeezed her husband's hand, Daphne was certain she was merely dizzy with love and desire.

The morning came quickly on the heels of too little sleep. In the quiet little rooming house, Raymond prepared to head back to Camp Shelby, about eight miles south of town. As he sat on the edge of the bed and pulled on his thick, Army-issued socks, he told Daphne about his friend John Cartmill from Lafayette, Indiana. "His girlfriend, Pauline Dunk, is coming to visit in a few days and he'd like the four of us to get together."

"Oh, good!" Daphne exclaimed. She was full of questions. "What do you know about her? Have you met her? Do you know how old she is?"

Raymond smiled at her enthusiasm. "I've never met her, just seen the picture that John keeps in his wallet. He sure is crazy about her." After a pause, Raymond added, "I guess she's about your age. She seems to be a very social gal; likes to get out and go places. John once said she never meets a stranger. In fact, she sounds a lot like you, so you two should get along just fine."

"Where does she live? Does she have a job?"

"Well, I'm not sure where she lives, but it must be somewhere around Indianapolis. I know she works in an office because John said something about her asking her boss for time off so she could make the trip."

Daphne smiled but said nothing more. It would be nice to have another woman to chum around with while the men trained.

Indeed, when Pauline arrived, the two women quickly became friends. Pauline was about Daphne's height, but fuller-figured. Daphne thought the extra weight suited her perfectly. A little flirty, Pauline had a delightful sense of humor that made her eyes dance. She told Daphne she had grown up close to Lafayette, Indiana, in a little town called Rossville. She now lived in Indianapolis and worked as a secretary at the Indianapolis Power & Light Company on The Circle.

During the day, the women acquainted themselves with the streets and shops of Hattiesburg. In the evenings, with the men off duty, the foursome took long walks around town, sometimes dining with other military couples. Daphne particularly liked the Kansas City Steak House and the Merchant's Café.

Late one night at the steak house, Daphne remarked, "You guys look exhausted. We know you had a long day. What happened at Camp

Shelby today?"

John paused for a moment. "Well, this was one of those days where we marched and we marched and we marched." The tall, brown-haired man looked over at Raymond as if to confirm that it was okay to tell the girls. "I bet we walked close to thirty miles in all, wouldn't you say, Ray?"

Raymond nodded. "It was tough, but at least we're more conditioned for it now, not like during that first week of training. Back then, I thought my legs and feet were going to literally fall off at the end of the day. And sometimes I wished they would."

Raymond turned to Pauline. "Even now, on the days we march, we're up and walking by 3:00 a.m. and don't stop until late in the day, with only a few ten-minute breaks and a short lunch. It sure makes for a long, painful day."

"Hey, Raymond, remember when Johnny Morrisey got a charley horse in his calf after lights out? Woke up the whole troop. The poor fellow was jumping around, yelling, and making all kinds of racket."

Raymond laughed. "That wasn't the *worst* of it. The *worst* part was listening to him carry on about his sore muscles for the next three days."

Pauline looked concerned. "What other things do they make you do? Surely your training isn't all just marching. Do you practice shooting guns or anything like that?"

Raymond seemed to measure his words carefully. "Not yet, but we will soon. We're scheduled to be trained with the M1 on the firing range. We'll also have to learn to take the gun apart and put it back together in a certain amount of time, and be tested on that. I hear we're going to train with the 30-caliber and 50-caliber machine guns after that."

Daphne eyed Pauline across the table. The talk of marching and guns reminded her of the seriousness of the training and the reality of what was to come.

On Christmas Day, Daphne and Raymond spent the day alone. It was their last day together before Daphne went back to Lebanon. As she repacked her suitcase, she put away her unused snuggies. Unlike Indiana, the temperature in Mississippi had been mostly in the sixties and seventies. And although the mild weather had been welcome, it just didn't seem like Christmas.

That evening, stopping in one of the few coffee shops open on Christmas, Daphne and Raymond held hands and said grace.

After Raymond carved a piece of baked pork chop, he looked at Daphne. "Why the long face, sweetheart?"

"I'm not looking forward to going home tomorrow." Daphne played with a forkful of mashed potatoes. "It's just not the same there without you."

"Well, why don't we just make plans for you to come back in a few months? I mean, if our unit is going to be training at Camp Shelby for several months, I don't see why you can't visit again. I've loved having you here this week."

Daphne cheered up at the suggestion. "What a great idea. I've had a wonderful time too, and I want to come back every chance I get. This week's weather has been unbelievable. I hear the temperature in Lebanon has been around 20 degrees all week."

"I don't miss that, do you?"

"Daphne shook her head. "No, not a bit." She added sugar to her coffee and stirred it. "Just for tonight, I'm going to pretend there *is* no war and that once you've finished training, you'll come home. We'll pick up right where we left off."

When You Come Home

Raymond laid his hand on Daphne's arm and gave it a squeeze.

Daphne dawdled while eating her meal, as if she could somehow stall the passing of time that would bring her departure. She reflected on the past few years. Their time together had been one moment of joy after another. Even the embarrassing incidents from their courtship were precious.

A smile tickled the corners of her face. "Raymond," she said, "do you remember when we were dating?"

Sipping on a soda, Raymond said, "Uh-huh."

"Well, the day you came and showed me your new car, I was wearing a black skirt. When I walked into the kitchen to get us something to drink I turned around and . . . "

Raymond's eyes danced. "Yes, Daphne, I saw your snuggies."

After the meal, the couple strolled arm-in-arm through the nearly deserted town. When evening came, they hailed a cab and rode around the streets of Hattiesburg, listening to the radio as it played *Let's Get Away From It All* by Frank Sinatra.

It was just the sort of playful tune Raymond always sang along with, but on this night he was silent. Daphne sensed her husband's growing melancholy, but felt helpless to do anything about it. This was one time when she wished she was gifted at singing. She'd pull her husband's head onto her lap and cuddle him as she would a baby, and she'd soothe away his hurt with a soft lullaby. Then she'd kiss his precious face over and over again….

Raymond interrupted her thoughts as he drew her closer and stroked her hair.

Despite their somber mood, tears didn't fall until Daphne heard

Bing Crosby's voice on the radio. She laid her head against Raymond's chest, wondering if they would ever share a truly happy Christmas. A merry, joyous, *white* Christmas . . . just like the ones she used to know.

When You Come Home

14

Early 1943

Albert Abston walked from room to room through the little white, wood-framed house on Green Street, tugging on chains to illuminate the overhead lights. Each time the room lit, he released a low, satisfied chuckle. Daphne followed him through the house, amused at her father's wonderment.

Though they would miss country living, her parents had finally bowed to the inevitable and decided to give up the farm they could no longer physically or financially maintain. Now, for the first time in their lives, they would have a home with electricity.

"Well I'll be," her father muttered when he discovered a light inside a closet. "Who would've ever thought..."

"Doesn't the house feel nice and warm, Dad?"

"Mmmm?"

"The house. It must be chock full of insulation. It's not drafty at all like our country place. Now we won't have to freeze on windy nights. Maybe we can even get rid of those old kerosene lamps."

Albert pulled the chain on the closet light twice more and then closed the door. "I reckon we'd better keep a couple just in case," he said. "I'm sure the wind blows down city streets too."

The warmth of the new house was a welcome change. But nice as it was, it seemed to make venturing outdoors to the privy even more dreadful. Once they were settled in the new quarters, Daphne decided it was time her parents enjoyed the convenience of indoor plumbing. Working longer hours, she increased her weekly earnings until she saved enough money to outfit a proper facility. Her father enlisted a neighbor to help construct a small addition on the north end of the house. Within weeks, the bathroom was finished, complete with a porcelain pedestal tub that Daphne had purchased second-hand from a family down the street.

What a treat to bathe with hot, running water. Daphne couldn't get enough of soaking in the huge tub.

"Your skin's going to rub off, child, if you don't quit taking so many baths," fretted her father one evening. Daphne only laughed, for her mother had told her that more than once she had come home from the grocery to find Albert luxuriating in an afternoon soak.

After her bath each evening, Daphne would bid her parents good night and retreat to her room. There she would write Raymond and keep him informed about life in their hometown:

January 17, 1943

Mrs. Shook (she insists we call her Lera) is such a sweet woman to work for, darling. It's still a shock how suddenly Mrs. Davidson died, but Mrs. Shook (I mean, Lera), is indeed a treasure.

When You Come Home

January 23, 1943

Dad and Mother are finally getting used to the idea of living in town, and the neighbors have been quite nice to all of us. But I know Dad still misses Pet and Daisy and the other animals, even if he doesn't miss the feedings and the cleanup.

January 30, 1943

Mary is now working at Winkler Manufacturing in Lebanon. With so many men headed off to war, there were several openings, so Mary applied and was hired right away. She is being trained on operating the cutting machine. She hopes to join the Winkler Choral Group later on.

February 11, 1943

Guess what, Raymond? Twyla had a healthy baby boy and she named him Johnny. I sure hope his papa gets a furlough soon to come and meet his new son.

February 20, 1943

Bernice and Clarence are moving back to Lebanon soon. It will be so nice to have my big sis close by. Clarence was classified 4F because of his persistent stomach ulcers, but even though he can't serve in the army, he wants to make a contribution to the war effort. So he's leaving teaching and working for a while at the gas turbine plant in Indianapolis. Bernice has been offered a high school teaching position at Perry Central.

February 25, 1943

Got a letter from Jack today, but it was very brief. He seems able to say so little of what he's actually doing in the signal corps. He keeps sending money to Mother and Dad, but of course they won't spend it. Instead they deposit it into an account for Jack. Won't he be surprised when he comes home?

Raymond wrote back nearly every day, describing his rigorous training exercises and his buddies. Daphne smiled when he wrote how the guys teased him about staying in camp night after night writing love letters to "the little wife back home."

I guess they just don't understand, sweetheart, what it's like to have someone like you waiting at home. I wish they could know how comforting it is, but, of course, they can't. There's only one you.

As winter began to release its grip on Lebanon, Daphne decided it was time her husband had a homemade treat, so she got up two hours early one morning and baked an applesauce cake. Since it was such a moist concoction, she felt sure it would stay fresh if she mailed it right away and packaged it tightly. Before she boxed it up, she picked up the letter she had written the night before to be included in the package. As she sat at the table rereading what she had written, the radio played *I Had the Craziest Dream* by the Harry James Orchestra. Daphne sighed, thinking of all the times she had dreamed of Raymond in the last few months. Her dreams were now treasured memories that grew fainter with time.

Picking up a pen, she added: *You are ever in my thoughts and prayers, dear, and in my sweetest dreams too.* She set the pen down and turned off the radio. She noticed how warm the music box was, not just because it had been playing, but because it was targeted by the sunlight that had pushed through the window and landed on the table. Looking out into the bright morning sky, it occurred to Daphne how much she missed hearing Raymond sing their special song. She picked up the pen again and added one more line to the letter.

P.S. You are my Sunshine!

15

Early Spring, 1943

The three months since Daphne's last visit with Raymond seemed like an eternity, and despite all the hometown activity, she missed him sorely. Whenever he called from Mississippi he usually tried to remain cheerful, hiding his feelings to spare hers. But one night his loneliness got the best of him.

"Oh, sweetheart," he said, "Lebanon seems so far away that it might as well be on another planet. Sometimes I ache so much to hold you again that I'm tempted to just come home..."

"Oh Raymond, you mustn't do that."

"I know, Daphne. Of course I wouldn't. But there are days when I wish I could hitch a ride back to Boone County and kidnap you."

"And where would we go?"

Raymond was quiet for a moment. "I'm thinking."

Daphne's voice held a teasing tone. "Well, if we're pretending, let me suggest an old country church or an abandoned barn."

"Up in the hayloft. No one would think of looking for us there."

"I wouldn't go up there unless you scared off the mice and got rid of the cobwebs."

Raymond was quick with his reply. "I promise you'll be comfortable. I'll bring fried chicken and a big box of chocolates."

Daphne was glad to hear her husband making light of the situation, but there was still a bittersweet tone to his voice. "Raymond, I have an idea. Instead of hiding out in Indiana, why don't I come to Mississippi? We can spend Easter together."

"Could you? I mean, will Mrs. Shook—Lera—let you take time off?"

"I've already discussed it with her. She knows the arrangement I had with Mrs. Davidson and it's all right with her as long as we get our customers taken care of."

Two days later, suitcases packed and workload rescheduled, Daphne headed for the bus station. This time, Jim Stout's wife, May, accompanied her on the long trip to Mississippi. During the daylight hours, the girls chatted as the bus slowly took them from state to state.

"Jim's rented a room in a downtown hotel," May said. "It'll be just like a second honeymoon."

Daphne swallowed hard, thinking of her own brief honeymoon in northern Indiana. After a while she said, "I hear the townsfolk in Petal, Mississippi have been encouraged to rent out spare rooms to visiting servicemen and their wives."

"Where is Petal?"

"Oh, not far from Hattiesburg. Just a few miles to the northeast. Raymond tells me he got us a room there in the Methodist parsonage."

It was well past sundown when the bus finally rolled into the station at Hattiesburg. Raymond was waiting and greeted the ladies enthusiastically just as Jim Stout arrived to meet May. After the Stouts set out for their downtown hotel, Raymond hailed a taxi for the short ride to the parsonage on South Main Street in Petal.

Inside the cab, Daphne snuggled as close as possible to her soldier husband and tilted her head to meet his lips. Their kisses were long and sweet.

"Ummm," Daphne murmured. "I've missed that."

"Me too," Raymond replied, his eyes promising much more.

Daphne framed his face with her hands. "I love you, Private Kelley. Do you know that?"

He nuzzled her neck tenderly and murmured, "I just might need some convincing tonight, my dear."

After a while, Daphne caught her breath. "I'm really curious about the place we're staying."

Raymond released her with a sigh. "I don't want to talk about that now."

"Well, we're almost there and—"

"And you want to know more about the parsonage?"

"Only if you want to tell me." Daphne tried to look coy as she sat up and combed her hair again. "Will there be other soldiers from Camp Shelby staying there?"

Raymond nodded. "I'm sure there will be. I hear it's a small house, but the family makes good use of every bit of room." The cab slowed to a stop. "We're here."

Daphne stared through the window at the one-story, white framed bungalow barely fifty yards away. "My, this *is* a busy place. Look how all the windows are lit up."

"They must have electricity all over the house," Raymond observed as he opened the car door for Daphne and handed some bills to the driver. Once outside, the couple gathered their luggage. They had taken only about a half-dozen steps when the front door of the house swung open.

"Come in, come in," said a tall man Daphne assumed was the minister.

"I'm Arthur O'Neil and this is my wife, Louise."

Daphne smiled and looked the couple over as she trailed Raymond into the house. They appeared to be in their late thirties, and their disparity in height mirrored herself and Raymond.

"Thank you for letting us stay with you," Daphne said, seeing the house overflowing with people.

Louise O'Neil had a gentle, motherly smile. "We're glad to have you both."

Reverend O'Neil cleared his throat. "We've had a slight mix up in sleeping arrangements, I'm afraid."

Daphne looked over at Raymond, eyebrows slightly raised.

The minister continued. "Nothing that can't be worked out, mind you. Two of our guests missed their train this afternoon, so they'll be staying with their husbands one more night. Unfortunately, we'll have to ask the two of you to sleep on the living room floor tonight. But in the morning, we'll move you to one of the guest rooms."

Daphne saw the disappointment in Raymond's eyes. They had been apart for months and now the long-awaited joy of their reunion night had been ruined. She reached over and squeezed his hand.

Mrs. O'Neil did her best to soften the blow. "Don't worry, we have extra blankets. We'll make you as comfortable as possible."

Raymond was silent for a moment, then said, "Could we move the sofa over a bit to give us some privacy?"

"Oh absolutely," responded the Reverend.

Relief washed over the preacher's wife's face. "Thank you for understanding." Mrs. O'Neil surveyed the living room and dining room crammed with noisy, laughing servicemen and their wives. "As soon as things settle down, we'll get you taken care of. Why don't you put your suitcases in the corner." She nodded toward a small square of space just beside the front door. "There's a large pot of coffee and a tray of homemade cookies on the dining room table. Please help yourselves."

"Thank you," Raymond replied, distracted by a thump on the shoulder.

"Hey, buddy!" Raymond called out as he turned and clasped another man's hand. "Daphne, this is Clinton Shaw. We train together at Camp Shelby."

Clinton was slim and even taller than Raymond. He bent down and took Daphne's hand. "Well hello, Miss Daphne. I feel like I know you already. Ray talks about you all the time and I do mean *all the time*." His eyes twinkled. "But that's alright. I've been known to mention my fiancée's name a time or two, myself."

Daphne liked Clinton immediately and could see that he and Raymond shared a special camaraderie. She wondered what his fiancée was like and if she ever came to visit.

Later, Daphne tapped Raymond's shoulder. "I'm hungry, honey. Let's have some refreshments."

They filled a couple of cups with coffee, helping themselves to some of Mrs. O'Neil's chocolate chunk cookies. Distracted by the noise, Daphne leaned closer to Raymond and lowered her voice. "How long do you think all these people are going to be hanging out in our sleeping quarters?"

Raymond looked glum. "I'm afraid they might be here for quite a while, so we'll have to make the most of it. They can't get out of here too soon to suit me."

When You Come Home

Munching on the cookies, they circled the room, chatting with Clinton and some of the other soldiers and their wives, making many new acquaintances. As midnight approached, Daphne became aware that the room had almost cleared.

"Let's call it a night, Mrs. Kelley," Raymond whispered into her ear. "I'll get our suitcases."

Moments later, Raymond and Daphne dragged the quilts provided by Mrs. O'Neil to an area behind the couch. It didn't matter that the space was cramped and the floor hard, despite the padding. The soldier and his wife found solace beneath the covers as they melted in the warmth of each other's arms. They surrendered their privacy for one more night of silent ecstasy.

The next morning, Clinton Shaw's fiancée, Bessie Maria Sardella, breezed in from Buffalo, New York. With her olive complexion and stylish clothes, she looked like a movie star to Daphne. The young high-spirited Italian girl moved confidently and talked rapidly, describing a New York Daphne could only imagine from what she had seen in the movies. It sounded like such a different world than central Indiana.

In the afternoon while the men were on the front porch talking, Bessie grabbed Daphne and said, "Mrs. O'Neil's running low on milk. Whaddaya say we go for a walk?"

To Daphne it sounded like a "wawk." She wondered if Bessie knew she had an accent, then remembered she, herself, had a Hoosier accent.

As they strolled north on Main Street, sheltered by large oaks, pines, and magnolias, Bessie described her wedding plans.

"Clinton and I had planned a June wedding. In fact, we've had it planned for nearly two years. We were going to be married in this gigantic church in Manhattan, but now with the world all topsy-turvy, we decided it was more important to be husband and wife than bride and groom."

"Oh, but you'll still be a bride, Bessie. And you'll be a beautiful one too."

Bessie blushed, but deflected the praise. Stopping at the corner of Main Street and Central Avenue, between the post office and a small school house, Bessie said, "Clearman's little grocery is this way." Daphne followed her west on Central until they reached the tiny Petal Market and Grocery Store at McKinney Street.

Inside the store, Mrs. Clearman greeted them cheerfully, directed them to the milk, then rang up the sale. Daphne looked down at the order pad on the counter and chuckled as she read the upside-down slogan: *We feed both man and beast.* Mrs. Clearman handed the change to Bessie and wished the women a good day.

Heading back toward the parsonage, Bessie stopped and turned to Daphne.

"Anyway, Daphne, I've been thinking . . . how would you and Raymond like to stand up with Clinton and me?"

It caught Daphne by surprise and she stammered a bit as she said, "Oh, Bessie, that would be wonderful, but are you sure? I mean, we really just met."

Bessie nodded enthusiastically. "I feel like I've known you forever. I guess it's because you remind me of my best girlfriend, Mary Claire. Same easygoing personality, same smile, same laugh. She's a very tiny girl, too, just like you."

Bessie started walking again. "If I had known you back home I'm sure you would have become one of my best friends, Daphne. So won't you please be my matron of honor?"

"Of course I will, Bessie."

When You Come Home

From behind them a car horn sounded. A four-door black Ford pulled up alongside them and Mrs. O'Neil leaned her head out the car window. "I'm heading home, girls. Would you like a ride?"

Both women squinted into the bright sunshine and shook their heads. "It's such lovely weather, I think I'd rather walk," Bessie admitted. "How about you Daphne?"

"I need the exercise too, but if you wouldn't mind taking the milk back with you, that'd be great, Mrs. O'Neil."

The minister's wife took the bottles from the women and thanked them for their thoughtfulness. She looked up at the sky, shaking her head. "I don't know, girls," she drawled, "it looks like rain to me." Pausing only for a moment, she put the sedan in gear and drove on.

Daphne looked again at the sky, then at Bessie. "Well, there's not a cloud to be seen."

Ten minutes later, the drops started falling from a quickly assembled congregation of clouds. Sporadic, unintimidating sprinkles fell at first but then the wide Mississippi sky darkened, the wind picked up, and a torrent gushed forth.

When the women reached the front porch of the parsonage, they started ringing out their long skirts. Over Daphne's laughter, Bessie said, "Do you think Mrs. O'Neil had some special insight into the weather?"

"What do you mean?"

Bessie rolled her eyes heavenward. "Just that maybe she gets her weather forecasts straight from the Source."

The following morning in a simple ceremony in the parsonage, Clinton Shaw and Bessie Sardella were married, with the Kelleys standing beside them. Surrounded by servicemen and their wives, the Reverend O'Neil officiated while Mrs. O'Neil stood dutifully beside him.

After the wedding, the bride declared, "Okay, everyone, let's head outside for pictures."

The day was dry, but the sudden rain the day before had left a coldness in the Mississippi air. Clutching her camera, Bessie yelled. "I want a picture of my new best girlfriend and her man."

Before Daphne knew what was happening, Raymond picked her up and swung her high up on his chest. With a cocky grin, he yelled, "We're ready!" Laughing, Daphne held on to her hat as Bessie snapped the picture.

After Daphne playfully struggled with Raymond, she demanded that he put her down. She took the camera from Bessie and snapped pictures of the bride and groom, as well as the O'Neils and their bored-stiff youngsters.

Later inside the parsonage, Daphne couldn't help watching the newlyweds. Sitting in a corner alone, they had eyes only for each other and seemed to believe they were hidden from the crowd. But Daphne knew exactly where they were—in the most wonderful place in the world.

A place called *Love*.

Since they now had a room of their own, Daphne enjoyed staying with the O'Neils and found great comfort in the pastor's Easter message. He spoke of Christ's love for all mankind, and how His resurrection was proof that true love endures, no matter how empty, lost, or abandoned a person might feel.

The O'Neils certainly made Daphne feel at home, and her stay in Petal was so enjoyable that in the midst of all the laughter and camaraderie, it was easy to ignore the fierce war raging across the ocean. But their pleasant respite soon came to an end. Late the following week, the men packed their belongings and headed back to Camp Shelby. From there they would journey to California for maneuvers. As sad as she was to be starting yet another separation, Daphne was sadder still for Bessie. Her wedding bliss had been abbreviated by the realities of war.

16

Spring, 1943

Back home, time seemed to crawl. Of course, the continued fighting overseas remained the hot topic. Citizens in Lebanon had a lot of different opinions about America's role in the war and felt free to expound upon them.

One day Daphne was shampooing Elberta Throckgilder, an older, unmarried lady. As Daphne made small talk about the war, from beneath her crown of thick lather, the woman declared, "Well, I just feel like you girls ought to stay home instead of chasing after your husbands. You're creating crowded conditions in the camp towns and spending all your money."

Daphne pushed the old woman's head further down into the sink, and dug her fingers roughly into Mrs. Throckgilder's scalp as she scrubbed. She wanted to say, "Who asked you? It's none of your business, you old biddy!"

"Daphne."

It was the voice of Lera Shook, and in Lera's eyes was a gentle, unspoken message that came through loud and clear: *Don't let her get to you.*

Daphne relaxed, rinsed out the shampoo, and sullenly turned off the faucet. Ringing the excess water from the old woman's hair, Daphne pulled Mrs. Throckgilder upright and wrapped her head in a towel—tightly.

Several nights later, Daphne sat at the old kitchen table in the Abston's kitchen enjoying a cup of strong black coffee and reading the nightly newspaper. On the third page, a poem caught her eye. It was titled, *When You Come Home.* Smoothing the paper flat, she read the poem several times. Despite the warmth of the coffee, the poem gave her a chill.

When You Come Home

When you come home, come home once more to me.
It is unlikely, dear that I shall be
Articulate. The words I've wanted so
To say, I'll try in vain to speak, I know;
I shall reach blindly for you, stricken dumb
With swift and aching joy when you come.

Or if my tongue find utterance at all
It will be commonplace and trivial.
But you will understand and, oh, once more,
I'll feel your hand laid lightly on my hair
As was your wont, smoothing it again
And yet again. You'll lift my face and then

We shall forget all else. You'll hold me fast.
When you come home, Come home to me at last!

When You Come Home

17

Late Spring, 1943

It was the Saturday before Memorial Day. The Ione Beauty Shop was closed for the holiday weekend and Daphne was enjoying the day off. Though the temperature had barely reached 60 degrees, the clouds were thinning and the sky promised a warm and pleasant day. Daphne had forced herself out of bed early to write a ten-page letter to Raymond. Now she sat at the kitchen table with her father enjoying one more cup of coffee. Drinking slowly, she savored every sip, appreciating the slightly bitter taste even more now that the sale of this precious commodity was restricted. Coffee and sugar were both scarce too, and Americans were allowed only a limited supply each week. Since Bernice and Clarence didn't drink coffee, they generously donated their coffee rationing stamps to Daphne and her parents. In exchange, Daphne often purchased tea bags for the Roberts.

In addition to limiting certain foods, the government was trying to curb excess driving and money spent on gasoline. So now all families had been issued coupon books for rationing of gasoline as well.

To do her part, Daphne spent her time walking more than eight blocks to the beauty shop from her parents' home. She enjoyed the exercise, but wondered how long her shoes would hold up. She had purchased the brown oxfords made especially for nurses last year after being advised by Mrs. Davidson that the thick rubber soles would cushion her feet and ease the strain of standing for long hours. Her boss had been right. Though the shoes were not stylish, they were so comfortable Daphne wore them almost constantly, except to church on Sunday mornings.

She propped her size four-and-a-half foot onto the empty chair at the end of the table and examined her pump. "I need to get these shoes repaired," she said to her father. "The soles are pulling away at the sides." She lowered her foot and took another sip of coffee. "I think I'll stop by the shoe repair shop this afternoon."

She wished she could simply go buy a pair. But new shoes were in short supply now that each person was allowed only two pair per year. Daphne wondered how her friend Bessie Sardella Shaw was faring with such restrictions. Bessie loved shoes and had a closet full. But for herself, two pair would be enough.

Maggie came into the room, wiping her hands on her apron. "I have a grocery list started. When you're downtown later today, would you pick up a few things for me? Unless you plan to walk, that is."

"I'll take the car if we need several things. I couldn't carry everything in my arms. Would you get the ration book out now, Mother? I don't want to forget it. And I must remember to take the sugar coupons."

The first time Daphne took ration stamps to Milo's Market, an uncomfortable feeling had settled over her as she carefully counted out the colored stamps for the grocer. But as she adapted to the new way of shopping, she was able to shorten her time at the market by planning her purchases and tearing out the required stamps ahead of time.

Daphne stirred her coffee and then took a sip. "What's on your schedule today, Dad?"

When You Come Home

Albert laid down his pencil, sat up straighter, and rubbed his right shoulder thoughtfully. "I'm going to plant us a garden."

"Really?" Daphne liked the idea. "You mean a victory garden?" She reached over and picked up the May issue of *McCall's* magazine lying on the table. She flipped through it until she came to page 80. "Look, Dad." She pointed to a half-page advertisement. "It says you can order a loose-leaf binder filled with pamphlets containing all kinds of information and tips on how to successfully grow a victory garden."

Albert Abston frowned. "That's for city folks. I already know how to plant a garden, child."

Daphne teased him. "Well, just the same, I thought sure when we moved to town, you'd put away your gardening tools and take it easy."

Albert nodded, his expression brightening. "Well, that *was* my plan. But the government wants people to grow their own fruits and vegetables for a while and help out the community. It seems like the right thing to do, so we can save the canned produce for the soldiers, like Raymond and Jack."

Daphne nodded encouragingly. "I think this is a good idea, but do you think we have enough space?"

Her father let her in on his decision. "There's just enough room on the west side of the house in front of that old shed. I've staked out a 12 by 15 foot section. Even though the garden will be small, I know I can harvest plenty of fruits and vegetables for our family. And we'll probably have enough for some of our neighbors as well."

Daphne eyed the colorful seed packets scattered across the tabletop: Danover carrots, Little Marvel peas, Early Scarlet radishes. "You've got a good variety, Dad. Do you have everything else you need?"

Albert thought for a minute. "I think I'm all set. Just need the good Lord to provide some sunshine and rain. In the right doses, of course."

Daphne stood up, stretched, and looked out the kitchen window. "What a gorgeous day. After being cooped up in the beauty shop all week, I could use some fresh air. I'll help you, Dad."

Mr. Abston smiled. "Oh, that's music to my ears, honey. I sure could use your young, strong arms. If we get started now, we should be able to finish up in time for you to do your shopping."

Father and daughter spent the morning tilling, planting, and carefully distributing rows of tiny seeds in the little patch of land behind the house. As she worked, Daphne felt proud knowing she was helping the war effort in a tangible way. She continued to think of all the changes on the home front and the sacrifices abroad due to the war. In her heart she knew the fighting wouldn't last forever. And despite the mostly negative consequences of war, she noticed a revived sense of camaraderie among her neighbors and friends as they pulled together in support of their nation.

Such patriotism was noble, but it was also the only way to survive emotionally, for there was really no way to escape the war. News of the fighting was so pervasive it seemed to echo in the night winds even when the sounds of the day had fallen silent.

When morning came and the radio was turned on, even the popular music embraced the worldwide conflict. From "Praise the Lord and Pass the Ammunition" to "Good-bye, Momma, I'm off to Yokohama," sounds emanating from the radio reminded Daphne of the closeness of war and her distance from Raymond.

Strangely, it seemed to Daphne her only refuge was in the letters she wrote to her husband. By focusing on what was happening at home, she could, if only for a few moments, forget what was happening in the world beyond Lebanon, Indiana.

When You Come Home

June 1, 1943

It'll be so nice, honey, having your family in town now that they've sold the farm. It's such a quick little trip over to Fordice Street that I can stop in whenever I want. I just hope I don't wear out my welcome with your folks...

But sometimes even the news from home took its shape from the fact that Raymond and his buddies were in training to join the war.

June 7, 1943

I got a phone call from Pauline last night. I'm sure John told you they got married while he was on leave. Pauline has moved back to the Lafayette area and is looking for a waitressing job. She promised to come see me in a few days and fill me in on all the details. Oh honey, I wish you could get a leave soon too. I miss you so much, especially with our first anniversary just a couple of weeks away.

P.S. You are my Sunshine!

18

Late June, 1943

My Dearest Darling Daphne,

Hi Sweetheart. Greetings from sunny, hot California. Sorry I haven't been able to write for a few days. We've been on maneuvers, training in the desert, and guess what? We got lost. No one seems to know how it happened, but it was really embarrassing. We wandered around for several days before finally making it back to camp. Of course, the guys from the other units teased us unmercifully and played jokes on us for several days.

Aside from that calamity, California has been quite interesting. Several of us guys just got back from a weekend pass to Hollywood. Guess what? We got to see them making a movie called Buffalo Bill. We even met Joel McCrea (he's quite tall) and got his autograph. I wish you could have been there to share the experience with me!

You've probably discovered the phonograph record inside this package and are wondering what's on it. Well, sweetheart, it's me. While we were in Hollywood, we visited a recording studio and I made you this record. I hope you like it.

Please give my love to the folks and everyone back home. I miss you.

Love, Raymond

P.S. Thanks for the poem. I'm putting it in my wallet next to your lock of hair. Indeed, I promise that I will hold you fast when I come home, come home to you at last.

P.P.S. You are my sunshine!

Daphne placed the bright yellow record on her player, positioned the needle near the edge and watched it track toward the center. She sat on her bed, a smile on her face as she anticipated the reassuring words of her husband. But when Raymond's voice crackled through the speaker, emotion overwhelmed her and his words were drowned out by her sobbing.

Never had her husband seemed so far away—so unreachable.

Now it was as if Daphne herself was the one lost and wandering alone. Alone in a desert of deepening despair.

The war overseas continued to drag on. Newspapers declared that American and British forces were in the midst of strategic air bombing against Germany. Though it was difficult to truly understand what was happening on the other side of the ocean, Daphne felt she must keep abreast of the Allies' advancement. Always on her mind, of course, was a question that would not be laid to rest: *How much longer will it be before Raymond's unit joins the fighting?*

19

Fall, 1943

Raymond remained in California until the middle of October when his troop was transferred to Fort Dix in Trenton, New Jersey. At the end of the month, he telephoned the Abston residence and encouraged Daphne to come for a visit.

"John says Pauline's coming in a few days. Maybe you can travel together."

"Oh, Raymond. Of course, I'll come. Vera was just asking about you the other day. I'm sure she'll help me rearrange my schedule."

It always picked up Daphne's spirits when Raymond called. Though it seemed the recording Raymond had made in California amplified the distance between them, his telephone calls bridged that divide.

When their conversation ended, Daphne telephoned Pauline Cartmill, who agreed to meet her at the Indianapolis train station two days later. Again, Daphne wasted no time securing her travel arrangements and on November 1, she boarded the bus to Indianapolis. After arriving at the bus station, Daphne picked up her suitcase and set off at a brisk pace for

Union Station on Louisiana Street. Pauline was waiting at the station, and the two quickly boarded the eastbound train for Trenton.

"My first train ride," murmured Daphne as she settled in for the journey.

"Oh, I think you'll enjoy it, Daphne." Pauline spoke confidently. "I much prefer it over the bus." Daphne gazed at the scenery flying past her window. *Heavens,* she thought, *I've done more traveling in the past year than in my whole lifetime.*

As they pulled into the Trenton train station, Daphne spotted Raymond and John. She pounded on the window and waved, catching their attention. The men ran alongside the train until it snorted and hissed to a stop.

"Oh, sweetheart, I'm so glad you're here," Raymond whispered after giving his wife a lingering kiss. When they looked over at John and Pauline, they were still locked in a passionate embrace. Daphne and Raymond looked at each other and both said, "Newlyweds!"

When they had collected their bags and were on their way, the men explained that they had arranged for both couples to stay at a downtown rooming house. After a twenty-minute cab ride, they arrived at the two-story home. Mrs. Appledorn, a middle-aged, stern-faced woman, greeted them at the door and went over the house rules.

"The top floor is where you all will be staying. I try to do my part for the war effort by renting it out to servicemen and their families. For the most part, my guests have been very respectful and quiet. I expect that to be the case with you as well."

Mrs. Appledorn sighed heavily, as if her patriotism were an unbearably heavy load. "I'll show you to your rooms in a moment. My son and I share the downstairs quarters. He's not here presently because he works nights. So I expect you all to be quiet during the day so he can sleep."

"What is your son's name, ma'am?" Raymond asked.

"No need to get too familiar," she said. "Since my husband passed on, God rest him, my son is the man of the house. So, Mr. Appledorn will do quite nicely, thank you."

Daphne and Pauline spent as much time as possible away from the Appledorn residence. They soon learned, however, that the landlady's cool demeanor was not altogether different from some of the other Easterners they encountered. As they returned from breakfast one morning, Pauline lamented, "Oh, Daphne, don't you just get tired of never seeing a friendly face or having someone to strike up a conversation with?"

"As a matter of fact, I do," Daphne said. Then her face lit up. "And I'm going to do something about it. I'm going to speak to the next person I see."

She didn't have long to wait. Walking toward them were two very dignified looking middle-aged ladies in fur coats. Before she lost her nerve, Daphne said, "Good morning, ladies."

The women slowed their pace a bit and the one nearest the girls paused, raised her eyebrows and responded, "Yes. Well, how do you do?" The women then hustled themselves along as if they feared a conversation might erupt.

Pauline glanced back several times to find the ladies looking over their shoulders at them. She laughed. "They're trying to figure out who we are."

"Or more likely, what planet we're from," Daphne added. She grabbed Pauline's shoulders and with a look of entrancement in her eyes, said, "We are vis-i-tors from a strange and dis-tant land known in this gal-ax-y as the pla-net In-di-an-a."

Their laughter was continuous from that point on, and as they opened the front door to the rooming house an arm shot out to halt them.

"Shhh! My son is sleeping."

The day before Thanksgiving, Raymond and John ran practically all the way to the rooming house. Bursting into the little room he shared with Daphne, Raymond grabbed all ninety pounds of her and laughed as he swung her high in the air. "We're going home for Thanksgiving, sweetheart!" he exclaimed. "John and I both got a four-day pass."

"Yippee!" Daphne yelled, clapping her hands. As she kissed her husband, she could hear the "shhh" from downstairs.

After throwing their belongings into their luggage, the two couples tiptoed downstairs to bid Mrs. Appledorn farewell and settle the bill. John knocked on the landlady's door and Daphne whispered to Raymond, "I'm sure she'll be glad to see us go. Every time Pauline and I entered the house, she scolded us for laughing too loud."

Hearing the heavy shuffling of feet, the four of them stood at attention and watched as the door swung slowly open with a creak. Mrs. Appledorn's round face dropped like a fallen soufflé as she spied the packed bags.

"Oh, you're leaving. And just as I was getting to know you."

Hours later, the weary travelers stepped off the train at the Union Station on Louisiana Street in Indianapolis. Gathering their suitcases, they drug them one block east before turning onto Illinois Street for a short walk to the Greyhound bus station. As they stood in line to purchase their tickets, John turned around. His eyes registered alarm.

"Ray," he hissed. "I don't have enough money to get to Lafayette." Looking sick, John pointed to the sign displaying prices. "It's fifty cents to go to Lebanon, and another sixty cents to Lafayette. That comes to two dollars and twenty cents for Pauline and me. I've only got a dollar and seventy-nine cents to my name."

Raymond rolled his eyes and snickered good-naturedly. "Why didn't you plan ahead before leaving camp, Cartmill?" Raymond fumbled in his pants pocket and pulled out some change. "Here, let me help you out." But as he counted the handful of coins, his laughter faded. "Oops, we don't have enough either."

John leveled a "you're-no-smarter-than-I-am" look at Raymond, causing both men to chuckle.

Daphne glared in their direction. Why were they laughing? There was certainly nothing funny about the situation they were in now. Chilled by the night air and wondering how they were going to get home, she didn't attempt to hide her irritation.

"Raymond, what happened? I thought we had plenty of money."

"And I thought so too, honey," he mumbled.

"I just don't believe this is happening," Pauline fired at the men with dismay.

The two soldiers eyed each other sheepishly while Raymond tried to defend their mistake.

"I guess we were both so excited about going home for Thanksgiving that we didn't give enough thought to the details of the trip."

"But now what are we going to do?" moaned Pauline, biting her lip. She looked like she might start crying any minute.

Daphne felt close to tears herself. The excitement of the trip had suddenly vanished, leaving only fatigue and despair in its wake. She didn't want to spend the night in this neighborhood. Her dad and mother would be horrified. They didn't have enough money to make a long distance phone call or even buy a sandwich.

Raymond's face had an expression Daphne had never seen. He swallowed hard and ran his hand across his military haircut, as if brushing cobwebs from his skull. "I think we'd better just admit we're a little short on cash, and hope the guy in the ticket office will take pity on two soldiers and their wives."

John nodded. "It's worth a try." He nudged Raymond forward. "Turn on your charm, Kelley."

Striding over to the ticket counter, Raymond explained their predicament to the older man at the window, who didn't seem overly concerned about their situation. Things were not looking hopeful but after a few awkward moments of silence, the ticket handler's face finally creased into a grin as he studied the young soldiers and their weary wives. Nodding, he waved them aboard. After thanking the man profusely, the grateful couples gathered their luggage and boarded the bus.

As the lights of Indianapolis gave way to the darkness of barren fields to the north, Daphne leaned her head against Raymond's shoulder. She was so tired, but she wanted to stay awake and just enjoy being with her husband.

"Raymond."

"Hmmm?"

"Do you still have that poem I sent you?"

"Of course I do. Do you want to see it?"

"No, that's all right."

Raymond cleared his throat and said softly, "When you come home, come home once more to me, it is unlikely, dear, that I shall be articulate. The words I've wanted so to say, I'll try in vain to speak,

I know..."

Daphne raised up and looked at her husband.

"I shall reach blindly for you," he continued. "Stricken dumb with swift and aching joy when you come."

"Oh, Raymond, you..."

He stroked her red hair. "Or if my tongue find utterance at all it will be commonplace and trivial. But you will understand and, oh, once more, I'll feel your hand laid lightly on my hair as was your wont, smoothing it again and yet again. You'll lift my face and then we shall forget all else. You'll hold me fast. When you come home, come home to me at last!"

Daphne melted back into her husband's comforting embrace.

Still stroking her hair, Raymond whispered, "The poem is in my wallet right next to your lock of hair. But it's also in my heart, along with every moment we've ever shared."

20

Thanksgiving morning, 1943

Heaven.

It had to be heaven.

The aroma of turkey and dressing, ham, apple and pumpkin pie, and other Thanksgiving delights all swirled together, anointing the air with the heaven-scent.

It was late morning, but Daphne still lay in her husband's arms, savoring the feel of the strength of his chest, the gentleness of its rise and fall as it spawned the breaths which fell against her hair.

Yes, heaven.

In the kitchen a pan fell to the floor, splitting the soft murmur of voices for a moment. Daphne tried to gently ease herself from Raymond's embrace.

"Your mother said to get your rest," Raymond said without missing a breath or opening his eyes.

"Shhh. You go back to sleep. I just need to go help in the kitchen."

Raymond pulled her back close to him and tightened his arms

around her.

"Raymond, let me go. They need my help."

"No."

"But, it's getting late and—"

"And they will do just fine without you this time. The kitchen here is smaller than the country house, so there's no room for you anyway." Raymond softened his hold a bit, but still would not release her. "Come on, sweetie. I need you much more than they do."

Daphne sighed and settled into his embrace. She closed her eyes again and gave silent thanks for his strength, his protectiveness, and his presence in her life.

Her prayer was short . . .

The little house on Green Street was filled not only with the scent of Thanksgiving, but also the sights and sounds of family. Jack's father and stepmother, Chester and Mildred, were there with their children, eight-year-old Chelsea, three-year-old JoAnn, and one-year-old Joyce. Clarence, Bernice, Ruth and Earl were there as well. With Albert, Maggie, Raymond, and Daphne, the house was buzzing.

"This is a beautiful turkey," Ruth said.

"It certainly is," Raymond added. "And baked to perfection, Mother."

Maggie Abston blushed, pleased that her son-in-law used that name. Raymond buttered a roll. "By the way, Chester, how is Jack getting along in the signal corps?"

"Oh, he's doing fine. I'm not quite sure what they've got that boy doing since he's very hush-hush about it all—Mildred will you please pass the gravy—but I think he's doing quite well just the same."

"What about your brother Floyd, Raymond?" Mildred asked.

"Oh, he's been released from the service."

"Really? How did that happen?"

"Well, Daphne knows as much about it as I do, but his father-in-law, Joe Purdue, passed away this summer, and there was no one to take care of the family farm other than Floyd."

"Is that so?" said Chester.

Bernice intercepted the gravy boat as it continued around the table and poured some over her mashed potatoes. "Well, there are so many things that need tended to here on the home front. It'll just be so good when this whole thing is over so we can get back to life the way it should be."

"Praise the Lord," Albert said. "And pass the gravy, please."

The following Sunday, after services at the Milledgeville Methodist Church, Daphne and Raymond again shared another Thanksgiving meal, this time at the Kelley home on Fordice Street. Daphne had helped with the preparations this time, and as she chatted in the kitchen with Leona, Mary, Twyla and Frances, she couldn't help overhearing some of the male conversation in the front room. While the women discussed food, family, and faith, the men spoke of war.

As she peeled potatoes, Daphne studied her husband. He took it all in stride, confidently speaking and listening carefully while others voiced their opinions. While Guy Kelley was speaking, Raymond looked up and through the doorway to the kitchen, catching Daphne as she watched him. He blew a kiss and winked at her. Then he motioned her to join him.

Daphne set aside the paring knife and wiped her hands on her apron.

"I'll be right back," she said to Leona Kelley. Hurrying into the front room, she met Raymond and followed him out to the porch.

"Are you all right?" she asked once the door had closed behind them.

"I'm fine," he said. "I just needed to get away from all the talk of war."

Daphne understood and impulsively stood on tiptoe to offer him a kiss. Raymond pulled her into his arms and sniffed her hair. "Mmm. You smell like turkey and gravy and all sorts of good things."

Daphne laughed. "I'll take that as a compliment. Are you hungry?"

Raymond nodded. "Yeah, for lunch . . . and for you," he added in a whisper."

"Your mom has been up since five o'clock fixing some of your favorite dishes. Even oyster dressing. She sure is a fabulous cook."

Raymond patted his stomach. "I know. I'll be yearning for these wonderful home-cooked meals when I'm back in the barracks eating Spam or dried beef gravy on toast."

Daphne tried to be comforting. "I'll pack some applesauce cake for your trip."

"That would be great." They stood there in silence, encased in each other's arms until the chilly air caused Daphne to shiver. "Maybe we should go back inside."

Nodding his head, Raymond started to smile. But before the smile was in place, Daphne was certain she saw something else: a look of uncertainty. Perhaps even fear.

21

Early December, 1943

It had been difficult for Daphne to tell Raymond goodbye that Sunday evening after the gathering at the Kelleys. When he boarded the train for the trip back to Trenton, she felt certain it would be a long time before she would see him again. Surely he would be sent overseas soon.

But less than a week later, Raymond phoned and explained that a couple of fellows in the unit had been given eight-day furloughs, causing a delay in their embarkation. "Could you come back to Trenton for another visit?"

Daphne practically hung up on Raymond as soon as he said it just so she could make her travel arrangements. First she called Pauline Cartmill.

Her friend had just returned home from a busy day at work when Daphne reached her by telephone.

"I know it's the spur of the moment, Pauline, but would you like to come to Trenton with me to see the men?" Daphne didn't voice the

143

words, but they both knew that this could be the last visit before their husbands were shipped overseas.

There was a heavy pause. "Oh, Daphne, I'm sorry, but I can't get off work right now." The disappointment and sadness were rich in Pauline's voice. "But will you please give John my love and tell him I miss him so very much?"

Daphne frowned as she hung up the phone. She wasn't fond of the idea of traveling all that way by herself, but if that was how it had to be, she would manage.

So three days later, alone, Daphne boarded the train again for Trenton, New Jersey. It was rather unnerving traveling by herself state after state, especially in the darkness. But it didn't matter, really. The Lord kept giving her opportunities to be with Raymond and she was determined to make the most of them.

At the train station, Raymond took her in his arms and just held her in silence. Finally, he picked up her bag and they started walking from the station. He explained that the boarding house he had requested would not be available until the following night. Forced to stay in a downtown Trenton hotel that first night, they found themselves next door to a loud party. When Raymond left for duty at Fort Dix early the next morning, Daphne was left alone and frightened at the ruckus in the next room. Though she tried to block out the noise, she didn't get much sleep and was thankful when daylight finally came.

Later that afternoon, Daphne was lying on the bed in the hotel room propped up against the pillows, reading. Her eyes had become heavy and she was just about to close her book and take a quick nap when she heard a key turn in the lock. The door opened; it was Raymond returning early from training. His face betrayed a secret as he crossed the room and gathered her close.

When You Come Home

"What, Raymond? What is it?"

"Guess who's coming in from New York today?"

Daphne leaned back and searched his face. "Is Bessie coming?" Raymond smiled and nodded. "Clinton's on his way to the train station right now to meet her."

"Oh, that's wonderful news!" Daphne's green eyes sparkled. "But where will she and Clinton stay?"

"Well, not here, that's for sure," Raymond said. "Actually Clinton was able to book a room in the same boarding house that we're moving into tonight. He talked with the lady who runs the place just this morning. A room became available unexpectedly, so he reserved it right away."

Daphne sighed with contentment, her spirits instantly buoyed by the news.

Raymond checked his wristwatch. "The Shaws will meet us here in about an hour. We'll go to a restaurant for supper, then head for the boarding house." Raymond eyed the luggage sitting next to the bed. "Looks like you're already packed. You didn't want to stay here another night, did you, sweetheart?"

Daphne bit her lip. "I've been packed and ready to go since eight o'clock this morning."

After eating at a local diner, the Shaws and the Kelleys moved into Mrs. Carr's boarding house in downtown Trenton. No one seemed to know Mrs. Carr's first name, but that didn't matter to the house guests who filled the eight rented rooms.

After each day of training, the soldiers returned for dinner and an early bedtime. Then, at 2:30 a.m., they were up and headed back to camp for roll call. Once awakened, Daphne, Bessie and the other women had trouble falling back to sleep again. So each morning after their men left, they gathered in one room, sharing bits and pieces of their lives. They moaned about missing their men. Some of them spoke of having a hard time adjusting to the rigid schedules. After a time, however, Daphne grew tired of all the long faces and attempted to lighten the mood.

One of the ladies piped up, "We all sit around here sad and blue, and here comes Kelley to cheer us up."

But one night it was Daphne who needed consoling. When the men returned from camp, they all marched in as a group, except for Raymond. None of the men would even make eye contact with Daphne at first. Finally, when the women became aware that one of the men was missing, everyone quieted down. Daphne walked over to Clinton Shaw.

"Clinton, where in the world is Raymond?"

"I'm sorry, Daphne," he said. "Raymond won't be able to be here tonight."

"What do you mean, he won't be here? He has to be here. This is where he's supposed to be!"

"Clinton, what happened?" asked Bessie.

"Well, it's just that Raymond's group got into a little trouble is all. Some of the guys who didn't get passes did something to the latrines and, well, the whole group lost their privileges."

One of the other men spoke up. "Yeah, one of the guys put potatoes in the drain pipes. Made a whale of a mess. Oh man, you should've seen ol' Kelley. He was pacing back and forth, madder'n a hornet and—"

The soldier's wife jabbed him in the side.

"What? It was funny."

"It's not funny to Daphne," Clinton said, and at the sound of her own name, Daphne raced up the stairs, flung herself onto the bed, and cried until sleep finally rescued her from the heartbreaking disappointment.

When You Come Home

Heavy snow was falling in the early morning of December 15 as the men prepared one last time to head back to camp, this time for certain embarkation. The beautiful Christmas card scenery stood in stark contrast to the dejection that hung heavy in the air as the soldiers bid farewell to their wives.

Daphne pulled her husband close one more time. Thoughts, emotions, and memories flooded her mind so much it made her dizzy. She forced herself to breathe deeply and as she did, she took in Raymond's scent, so clean and strong and manly. His uniform also smelled clean, yet strangely stale and lifeless. She felt, really *felt* the strength of his embrace, and she noticed the drab green fabric of the uniform seemed ominously scratchy and stiff.

She wanted time to stand still, but it didn't. When Raymond finally pulled away from her she was sorry she had wasted these moments. She should have been looking deep into his eyes, basking in the love reflected there. She should have been cupping his strong jaw and soft cheeks in her hand, memorizing the feel of this man. She should have been delighting in his breath against her face, then kissing him and catching that breath. *To have and to hold, from this day forward.*

But when they did kiss, she forgot to breathe in. And then he was gone.

Only then did time stand still.

22

Mid-December, 1943

On the phone, Raymond's voice was strained. "Honey, I've developed a silly little cold and have been detained from my group. Can you believe it? They're going to be shipped overseas later on today *without* me."

Daphne's heart sank as low as Raymond's troubled voice. What a terrible disappointment for him to be separated from Company C. After all, he had trained with the group for more than a year and she was sure it had never entered his mind that his buddies might go on without him.

"Once I recuperate, I'll probably be sent overseas with the next unit."

"Oh, Raymond, I'm so sorry. I wish I could say something to make you feel better." But of course she couldn't. She knew his cold would get better in a matter of days, but she also knew from experience that the cure for loneliness and loss was a painfully slow elixir of equal parts time and faith.

When You Come Home

It was a bleak Christmas.

Separated from her husband and knowing he was alone and waiting to be shipped overseas, Daphne longed to be with him, if only for a few hours.

It wasn't to be.

Soon after the first of the year, Raymond boarded a ship headed for Northern Africa with the 45th Division, 179th Infantry.

23

January, 1944

After leaving work one crisp, sunny January day, Daphne passed by Haffner's Dime Store, noticing again the collection of Government stars in the window. She went inside and chose a silver one—signifying Raymond was now overseas—then headed home. Walking down the sidewalk on South Lebanon Street, Daphne noticed several homes with stars in the windows.

So many stars . . . so many families with loved ones in the war.

The stars were either blue or silver. Daphne didn't spot any gold stars, which would have signified the death of a beloved soldier.

She thanked God for that.

That evening, Daphne pulled down the blue star from her window. She remembered how emotionally spent she had been when she had first displayed the patriotic decoration. "Star light, star bright," she whispered as she had that first dismal night. But the tears which had finished her earlier refrain refused to fall. Had she grown that much stronger? Or did she simply have no more tears to give?

In town, her bedroom window faced the street. As she placed the silver star against the glass, she knew it would be visible to those who drove by. Once again she felt a sense of fellowship with others in the community. It was funny how a symbol could evoke such a strong emotional tie to others also making sacrifices.

"What are you doing, Daphne?" Albert Abston peered through the doorway, trying to see past her.

Daphne stepped aside. "I just replaced the blue star with a silver one."

Her father walked over and carefully inspected the new star. "This one means your soldier is overseas?"

"Yes. Have you noticed there are quite a few silver stars around town now?"

Albert nodded. "Clarence and Bernice took your mother and me for a ride the other day. We drove by several homes with stars in the window; mostly blue ones, but some silver. A lot of folks have been touched by this war in one way or another." He paused for a minute before turning to face his daughter.

"Have you heard from Raymond lately?"

"No." Daphne replied quietly. "I've read that his unit is moving toward Anzio Beachhead in Italy. It sounds like the fighting is ferocious there, Dad. Raymond is so far away and I'm really afraid for him."

"I know, honey. We're all concerned about Raymond. But that boy's got a good head on his shoulders. He'll be careful." He patted Daphne's shoulder. "Your mother and I will double up on our prayers. That's about all we can do."

Daphne nodded, choking back the lump in her throat.

"Good night, Daphne." Her father bent to kiss her cheek before he left the room.

Daphne readied herself for bed and climbed in, thinking about what her father had said. He was right, of course. Prayer *was* her only weapon, and each night she wielded it fiercely.

24

January, 1944

A noisy car on the street outside the house woke Daphne from her fretful sleep. She rolled over in the tangled covers, leaned close to her nightstand, and squinted to see the clock in the faint glow from the streetlight outside. Not quite six-thirty. Mercifully, the alarm wouldn't go off for another few minutes.

Daphne rolled onto her back and stared at the ceiling. As she focused on a pattern in the ceiling plaster, her thoughts turned to Raymond. Where was he right then? What was he doing? Was he safe? Was he afraid? Was he thinking about her?

Such thoughts were never far from her mind, and sometimes they nearly drove her mad. She threw off the heavy patchwork comforter—her dad kept the house very cool—and struggled to get up. Pulling the string, Daphne ignited the overhead light and climbed back beneath the covers for a few more minutes of warmth. Was Raymond warm? Was he comfortable, or was he lying on the ground somewhere in a thicket, waiting to fire on the enemy? Could he even *do* such a thing? Could he, in a moment of truth, even bring himself to take another man's life? Like Gary Cooper in the movie, *Sergeant York*, that Daphne had seen with her father, killing was so contrary to Raymond's beliefs.

The alarm rang. She silenced it and lay there a moment longer, staring at the ceiling. She made a mental note to dust away an intruding cobweb her sleepy eyes had spotted.

In the kitchen, her father was studying the paper. "Morning, Dad. Thanks for making the coffee."

"Mmmm." He looked up over his glasses which were perched halfway down his nose. "Good morning, dear. Did you sleep okay?"

Daphne came over to the table, set her coffee down, and kissed her father on the top of his head. "I woke up a few minutes early, just early enough to lay there and look at the dust. I'm going to clean my room tonight after work."

Albert lowered his paper. "Sometimes I think you work too hard, Daphne. It would do you good to relax."

Daphne sighed. "I know, Dad. But there's always so much that needs doing. And besides, staying busy keeps my mind off of things."

"I know, but I think tonight you ought to just relax in the tub. Forget about the dust for a day or two."

Daphne smiled. "I won't be able to relax as long as I know it's there, Dad. It won't take me long to clean up, and then I'll follow your orders and soak in the tub."

"Well, all right, Daphne." He disappeared behind the paper again and Daphne sipped on her coffee, her eyes drawn to the persistent front page headlines.

War, War, War!

When You Come Home

Work provided no escape from the news. In fact, it was all anyone ever talked about, no matter how many times Daphne tried to change the subject. By the time she headed home, Daphne was ready to do what her dad had told her; relax in the tub.

And she would, as soon as she had straightened up her room, dusted, and cleared away that cobweb.

Her parents were both dozing peacefully in the front room, so she tiptoed past them and into her bedroom. Hanging her purse on a hook on the backside of the door, Daphne took off her shoes and immediately set about to clean up her little corner of the world. She stared at the corner of the ceiling. The cobweb was gone. She looked for smudges on her mirror. They had miraculously disappeared. The clutter on the top of her dresser was nowhere to be seen. Neatly arranged, everything was in its place.

Dad, she thought. Although tempted to rush into the front room and give him a big thank you kiss, she decided to let him sleep. The best reward for him would be for her to relax in the tub.

Daphne reached into the dresser drawer and pulled out her nightgown. As she closed the drawer and headed for the bathroom, she was struck by an odd sensation. Something was different. Something was wrong.

She turned back and surveyed the room for a few moments. Everything was perfect. Everything was in its place.

Relax, she told herself.

Daphne ran the water in the tub as warm as she could stand. Steam rose up and she imagined being in a fog. She lay back in the water and basked in its gentle caress.

The necklace!

She sat upright in the water. That's what was wrong in her room— the candy necklace Raymond had given her was gone from the knob on the dresser.

Stepping out of the tub, she dried herself and put on her nightgown. Frantically, she searched everywhere, even beneath her pillow. The necklace had vanished.

"Did you have a nice bath, honey?" Her dad stood in her doorway, yawning.

"Dad, do you know what happened to the necklace that was hanging on my dresser?"

"I'm so sorry, Daphne, I was going to tell you. I must've knocked it off while I was cleaning. Anyway, it fell on the floor and pieces of it broke."

"Where is it now, Dad?"

Albert's face turned ashen. "It was shattered, so I threw it away. It went out in the trash this afternoon. Did I do something wrong?"

Even though she knew he had meant well, Daphne was barely able to keep from screaming. Another piece of Raymond was gone—a piece of their life together thrown away. She discovered her father had also sopped the movie-ticket birthday card when he was spraying the mirror. It, too, met the same fate. Now, as much as she loved her dad, she could barely even look at him. Was he losing his sense of reasoning? Didn't he know these souvenirs were as priceless as diamonds to her?

All during work the next day her resolve grew stronger. She would certainly not let any more mementos of Raymond slip through her fingers. After work, Daphne walked to Stark Stationery Store where she purchased a large black scrapbook and had Raymond's name inscribed on it in gold letters. As she carried it home, she thought of what could go in it. Her intention was to fill it with keepsakes and mementos from the war. Then later she could add pictures of the children she and Raymond would have someday.

Sitting alone at the kitchen table late that evening, Daphne sorted through the items she had already collected. Carefully, she inserted Raymond's birth certificate, a darling picture of him as a baby, and his church membership card. She hummed tunelessly as she glued their wedding license and pictures onto the pages, along with their marriage announcement from *The Lebanon Reporter*. The book couldn't be complete without Raymond's "Order to Report for Induction" into the Army, and pictures of him in dress uniform at Camp Shelby. She also included snapshots of their friends, the O'Neils and the Shaws.

Two other items were featured in the scrapbook: the recording Raymond had sent from California and the message he had so affectionately typed the day before his induction.

By the time she finished, it was very late and the house was deadly quiet. Carrying the scrapbook to her room, she looked for a safe place to keep it. She was certain her father would never throw anything of hers away again, but still, she needed a secret place.

In her drowsiness, she thought of Psalm 91.1: *He that dwelleth in the secret place of the most high shall abide under the shadow of the Almighty.*

Secret place. Shadow.

She looked around her room and noticed that the light from the street clung to her floor, but stopped short of her bed, which remained in the shadows.

Her secret place. She lifted the corner of the mattress and placed the scrapbook underneath. As she lay there awaiting sleep, she could feel the slight bulge made by the book beneath her. Raymond seemed closer to her now, and she slept peacefully, with all she had left of him.

PLEASE DON'T TAKE
MY SUNSHINE AWAY …

25

March, 1944

Despite the war and emotional unrest across the world, life in Lebanon, Indiana settled into a fairly normal routine. Daphne continued to work long hours at the beauty shop. Keeping busy seemed the best way to combat loneliness, and the fact that business in the beauty shop actually increased because of the war was a benefit as well. With men headed off to fight, women continued to step into some of the open positions in the workplace. Daphne's clientele included many women now employed in factories and businesses around town who simply didn't have the time to set their own hair.

On weekends, Daphne chose to stay close to home, tinkering around the house, writing letters, and helping her parents with chores. She continued to visit the Kelleys and other relatives, and saved her money for an occasional movie with friends. Though some gals partied excessively and hit the dance floor in droves while their men were overseas, Daphne had no desire for nightlife and steadfastly declined the invitations. She knew in her heart she couldn't enjoy such frivolous doings while Raymond was risking his life on a field of battle. In fact, it seemed unfaithful.

Every Sunday, Daphne loaded her parents into Raymond's aqua-blue Ford Coupe and headed for the First Baptist Church in downtown Lebanon. The stately two-story brick building had been built in the 1800s and stood on the corner of Washington and East Street. It still seemed strange to walk into the sanctuary and not be greeted by Reverend Metz, but the kindly man had left the church last year and LaRue Jensen was now leading the congregation.

To honor members of the congregation serving in the armed forces, the church had prepared a poster listing all the servicemen and women. It hung downstairs in the classroom hallway. Daphne knew just where to find Raymond's name on the board.

During the worship service, Daphne sometimes glanced around the large sanctuary, her eyes falling on the empty spaces in the pews. She looked at the drawn faces of those she knew so well and realized very few families were untouched by the war. Many had sons, fathers, or husbands away in the service. Through his sermons, Reverend Jensen tried to encourage his parishioners, but Daphne understood the strain remaining on their faces. Just the night before, Daphne had read another passage from the Book of Psalms that struck a chord. She longed for a time when, indeed, *The righteous will flourish in an abundance of peace*, but wondered if that peace would ever come.

Although Daphne drew comfort from worshipping with her family and friends, it was difficult attending church without her husband. Even in the midst of the hundreds in the congregation, she felt lonely in the crowd.

When You Come Home

Daphne was home alone when she received an envelope from the United States Government. Hands that moments before had been steady now began to shake as her eyes skimmed over the enclosed letter. The message was brief. While fighting at Anzio Beachhead on the west coast of Italy, Raymond had been wounded.

26

March, 1944

T he Purple Heart awarded to Raymond was enclosed in the bulky letter. As Daphne cradled the medal in her palm, images of her husband lying injured on some French battlefield overwhelmed her. Looking for more answers, she read and re-read the message. Though it reassured her his injuries were not life-threatening, the letter was otherwise vague. She needed to know how Raymond had been injured—and where.

What she really wanted to know was, would her husband be sent home?

Oh Lord, please let him be sent back to get well.

Much later in the day, Daphne's parents returned home. Maggie became alarmed after a quick look at her daughter's ashen countenance.

"What happened, child?"

Daphne thrust the letter into her mother's hands. Albert leaned over his wife's shoulder and together they scanned the brief message, their faces tightening with concern.

When You Come Home

"Daphne, it's quite clear Raymond's life is not in danger," assured her father, the muscles in his face appearing completely relaxed. "He's apparently in some sort of field hospital and he's being taken care of by Army doctors and nurses."

All day long, Daphne had struggled to keep her wits about her and needed to hear her father's comforting words. She slowly nodded her head. "I *am* relieved and thankful Raymond is being cared for. But just knowing he's halfway across the world—who knows just where— wounded and without any family with him, is almost unbearable." Tears filled Daphne's eyes, a mixture of despair and hope. "Oh, Dad, do you think there's even a possibility they'll send him home?"

Albert's face showed compassion. "Well, the letter doesn't make any mention of that, honey. Come on, Daphne, you and Mother. Sit down here next to me on the couch. We'll pray."

Daphne lowered her tense body to one side of her father. Maggie sat quietly on the other. Albert reached over and gently covered his daughter's hand with his own. "Lord, you know our hearts are heavy right now. We ask that you be with Raymond, watch over him, and heal him. Please give him the peace of your presence. We also ask you to guide those taking care of him as well and provide them with the skill they need to bring Raymond back to complete physical and mental health. Please calm our fears as well, Lord. In Jesus' blessed name I pray, Amen."

Albert squeezed his daughter's hand as he reached into his back pocket for his handkerchief. "Here, Daphne. Wipe your tears, and remember God is watching over Raymond."

Though still concerned about her husband, Daphne knew her father was right. She was too far away to help Raymond. Only the Lord could do that now.

The days passed slowly as Daphne anxiously awaited more information. Nearly two weeks later, she received a V-mail card from Raymond. On the front he had skillfully drawn a deer eating in the woods. One look at the drawing assured her that her husband was all right mentally as well as physically, and she closed her eyes in thankfulness to God.

Along with the card was a letter explaining he had been hit in two different places in the right shoulder by shrapnel from a land mine. So limited was his explanation that Daphne still didn't know the name of the military hospital or the place where he was recuperating. He did tell her, though, he would not be sent home. He would rejoin his unit as soon as his recovery was complete.

During the weeks following, Daphne yearned desperately to be near her husband. If only she could help nurse him back to health and be sure he was receiving adequate care. She wondered about his frame of mind, praying his recovery would be complete. Several weeks later, in his next letter, Raymond assured her of his nearly-complete recovery and explained that he would be reunited with his unit around the first of May.

May 1st was a dark, rainy Monday in Lebanon. Daphne had just arrived home from work when she heard a knock on the front door. She opened the door to a smiling young man from the local florist. Nestled in his arms was a long white box.

"Well, what's this?"

The young man grinned widely. "Flowers for you, miss."

Daphne reached for the box and the attached card. Tearing open the small envelope, she read, *Happy Belated Easter from Raymond.* After fumbling with the box lid, she lifted out fifteen beautiful, perfectly shaped red roses. She smiled, knowing not only had her prayers been answered for Raymond's physical healing, but his love for her and his Christian faith were as strong as ever.

Several weeks later, Raymond sent word that he had rejoined his group. Like his previous letters, his tone was light. He wrote about two of his buddies, Bill Hicks, and a man from Cookeville, Tennessee named A.C. Clark. *After this war is over and I come home,* Raymond added, *I want you to meet these guys. I know you'll like them, sweetheart.*

Otherwise, Raymond skimmed over what was happening to him. Instead, he inquired about the latest news from family and friends. Daphne knew, however, from newspaper accounts that his unit was meeting up with the 3rd and 36th Divisions and would be heading through Southern France, en route to Germany.

27

Late Spring, 1944

As summer approached, Daphne continued her daily love letters to Raymond. It was her way of visiting with him across the miles. One night, she packed up another applesauce cake to ship across the ocean. Raymond's immediate response was: *Bless you, Mrs. Kelley! My cake arrived in a lot of crumbs, but tasted wonderful.*

Sometimes a couple of weeks would pass between letters from Raymond. Then Daphne would be rewarded with a huge pile of mail. Like clockwork, each weekday morning the middle-aged postman trotted into the salon, whistling a cheerful little tune. And answering his overture with a soft whistle of her own was the postman's wife who worked on the third floor of the same building.

The carrier always handed the mail to Daphne, since she was stationed closest to the door. "Your soldier shows me no mercy at all," he said, his breath ruffling his thick mustache. "All this weight is surely gonna break my poor back."

"Oh, stop complaining," Daphne said as she reached for the mail, interested only in her husband's familiar handwriting. "Hauling these letters around all day is good for you and you know it. Why, it'll strengthen your muscles so you can carry more mail tomorrow."

The postman shrugged and, with a twinkle in his gray eyes, trudged up the street, his whistle fading as he turned the corner.

One of Raymond's letters was lengthy and Daphne read it over and over, laughing more each time. It seemed Raymond's troop often fought alongside the British. At nighttime, they shared stories. Raymond wrote:

Daphne, the British love hearing a southern accent. A.C. and our other southern soldiers have made quite a hit with them. One night we were sitting around the camp and one of the southern boys began reciting a bit of rural doggerel to entertain the British soldiers. One man slapped his knee in rhythm and hollered, 'I've got a gal from Arkansas. She can chaw more tobacco than her Pa can chaw.' The guy continued with the story, but whenever he got back to that part about 'Pa can chaw,' the British soldiers just howled with laughter and slapped their knees. They asked for several encores the next day, bringing in other soldiers to hear. They always laughed at those lines the most. A.C. tells me that later that evening when he was on guard duty and most of the camp was asleep, one of the leaders of the British troops joined him to talk for a bit. I guess talk was just of daily things, but A.C. could tell this soldier, who had been one of the men who had gotten such a kick out of the story earlier in the day, had something on his mind. Finally, unable to contain himself, he turned to A.C. and blurted out, 'I say, Clark, what is a 'pockinchaw'?

On June 6, 1944, Allied troops attacked the coast of Normandy in what the newspapers dubbed the "D-day invasion." Commanded by General Dwight Eisenhower, six divisions—three American, two British, and one Canadian—participated in the attack on five separate landings. One hundred thousand men survived and made it to shore, but by the end of the day, over nine thousand soldiers had perished.

Later in the month, the papers announced a foiled attempt on Adolph Hitler's life by his own confidants. Amazingly, the Nazi ruler suffered only minor injuries. Daphne despised this evildoer who was trying to rule the world, attempting to play God and deciding who lived and who died.

28

August, 1944

As summer dragged on, Daphne and her father often had private discussions about the war. Attempting to follow Raymond's unit, Daphne read anything she could lay her hands on about the battles overseas. The local newspaper reported that Raymond's division was in the midst of heavy fighting in Southern France. Imagining the daily horrors her husband must be facing, Daphne read and re-read every bit of information he sent her way. But she didn't gain much insight, as he kept his letters cheerful to protect her from the ferociousness of battle.

In fact, some of his writing was downright hilarious and made Daphne laugh out loud. One hot, sticky Saturday evening, just before bedtime, she shared a letter with Albert and Maggie.

"Mother, Dad, why don't you put down your books for a minute and I'll read you some of Raymond's last letter. I think you'll get a kick out of it."

Albert lowered the heavy, worn Bible gently onto his lap and sat up straighter in his rocker. "Well, honey, you go right ahead. We're all ears, aren't we, Mother?"

Maggie nodded and pressed down the corner of the page of her book, marking her spot before placing it on the end table. She patted the couch beside her. "Sit down, Daphne. Looks like he's written several pages."

Daphne curled up next to her mother. "I'll skip over the first part."

Our wool uniforms are hot and pretty dirty from wearing them so long. The other day I just couldn't stand it any longer. I decided to give myself a bath, right there in the open. I told my buddies: 'This isn't going to be much of a bath, but I'm gonna take it! Everybody just turn your heads.' Someone yelled over to me, 'Kelley, are you going home?' I told him, 'I'd sure like to.' I took off my helmet liner, filled it with water, undressed, and used my undershirt for a wash cloth. Sure wasn't anything compared to soaking in that nice new tub at your folks' house, sweetheart, but it was the best bath I've had for a while.

Maggie reached over and patted her daughter's hand. "When that boy comes home, dear, we'll give him all the time he wants to soak in our tub."

"I'll bet he's counting on that, Mother. We sure take our luxuries for granted, don't we? But there's more here I want you to hear." Daphne found her place and continued.

After walking for hours one day, our platoon came upon a small pond. I decided we might be able to get us some fish for lunch. I set off a grenade in the water and, sure enough, up came some fish. With help from my buddies, we cleaned them and started cooking. Just then, the Germans started shelling. We didn't have time to think; we just ran for cover. Sure didn't know the enemy was anywhere within eight or ten miles of us. Anyway, by the time we returned later, our fish had been eaten. I was so mad at those Germans. I said to A.C., 'I hope they all get sick!

Albert chuckled. "Well, Raymond sure hasn't lost his sense of humor. We can be thankful for that." But even in the lightness of the moment, the seriousness of the situation was not lost on any of them.

Daphne carefully folded up the letter, closed her eyes, and rested her head against the back of the couch. She sighed as she felt tears rising, and said in a small, unsteady voice, "He must be in danger just about all the time."

Daphne's birthday in mid-August was a quiet affair—dinner with the folks, cards from the girls at the salon, and late that evening, a phone call from Bernice.

"Daphne, I have some birthday news for you," she declared. "I'm expecting a baby."

"Oh, Bernice, that's wonderful. When will the little one be here? What's Clarence think about the news? You know, we should probably start looking for baby clothes right away and—"

Bernice laughed softly at her excited little sister. "Well, it's a little early for buying clothes. I'm due sometime next spring; still a long way off. And you know the trouble I've had before. But Clarence is thrilled, of course, and we're quite certain I'll carry this child to term. Now, honey, why don't you put Mother on the phone?"

Daphne surrendered the earpiece to her mother.

"Oh, what wonderful news," Daphne heard her mother say. It was a welcome reprieve from the daily tallies of death overseas.

Shutting her bedroom door behind her, Daphne knelt beside her bed and prayed, not only for Raymond and the other Allied soldiers, but also for the niece or nephew growing inside her sister, that it might be born healthy and grow up in a world where death comes only at the end of a long life, well-lived.

THE OTHER NIGHT, DEAR,
AS I LAY DREAMING,
I DREAMED
I HELD YOU IN MY ARMS

29

Saturday, September 9, 1944

❝ Girls, let's all go out to dinner and a movie tonight, my treat," Lera Shook said near the end of a busy Saturday in the salon. Daphne caught a surprised glance between the other two girls, Annabelle and May. Although Lera had always been a kind employer, she had never before suggested socializing after hours. Now she was even willing to pay for it. Each girl had a loved one in the service—either still in the States or overseas—and the prolonged fighting was wearing on their spirits. In truth, Daphne would have much preferred to just stay home and rest. On Thursday, she had had two wisdom teeth removed and her gums were still quite tender and continued to throb. But she knew the other girls would insist she come along, so she forced a smile. "That's a great idea. A night out sounds wonderful."

Annabelle and May nodded in agreement.

So that evening the girls climbed into Mrs. Shook's car and made the long trip to Indianapolis. It was a pleasantly warm evening and despite the pain in her gums, Daphne felt her spirits lift during the ride. The ladies enjoyed some Chicken Velvet Soup in the L.S. Ayres Tea Room and then made their way to the Indiana Theater.

Since You Went Away was playing. Even though it dealt with what they were enduring—life on the home front apart from their husbands— the movie had received smash reviews, so the girls decided to see it. Daphne liked Claudette Colbert in the role of the mother, and it was fun seeing Shirley Temple as a teenager even if it was still hard to shake the image of her as a child in *The Good Ship Lollipop*. Though the family in the film was wealthier than Daphne's, she could relate to their emotions. In fact, by the end of the film, all four of the women ended up hunting for their hankies.

The movie was longer than Daphne expected—nearly three hours— and she was quite tired by the time they reached the car. On the way home, as the other girls chatted about the movie, Daphne remained quiet. After a moment of silence, Annabelle asked, "You all right, Daphne?"

Daphne smiled. "Oh yes, I'm fine."

"Are your gums still bothering you, honey?"

Daphne nodded. But she wasn't so quick to admit to a festering worry. She hadn't received a letter from Raymond in a few weeks. And though she knew he was at the battlefront and didn't have time to write, she had to constantly remind herself he would be all right.

God would see to that.

In bed, Daphne had trouble falling asleep. Her cheeks were still slightly puffy from the surgery and she could taste an occasional trickle of blood. She tried to take her mind off the pain by concentrating on what the rest of her body was feeling. Beneath the mattress she could sense the gentle nudge of the scrapbook. Pushing back the blanket, she got out of bed, lifted the mattress and pulled out the book.

When You Come Home

After pulling the cord to illuminate the room, Daphne sat on the bed and began thumbing through the pages. The mementos that chronicled her courtship and brief married life with Raymond, as well as his wartime experiences, comforted her.

She started at the end of the pages she had already filled. There was the V-mail card from Raymond, the one where he had drawn the picture of the feeding deer. There was the land mine marker Raymond had sent her to commemorate the cause of his battle wounds, and the Purple Heart he had been awarded. The recording Raymond had sent her from California was in the scrapbook too. She had listened to it only once, and now it was taped to a page, rendered silent. The scrapbook held photographs too: from Trenton, from Petal, from Hattiesburg; from their windy wedding day, and a picture of Raymond in his new uniform.

Daphne yawned, ready to put the book away, but she took a moment to read the letter Raymond had tapped out on the typewriter just before he went away:

I Love You Sweetheart. Dear Daphne, let not your heart be troubled. Ye believe in God, believe also in me. Love Raymond.

Comforted by the words, Daphne smiled despite the soreness of her mouth. She placed the book back under the mattress and then crawled between the covers and prayed: "Lord, you know I'm worried about Raymond. I haven't heard from him for a long time and that scares me. Please keep him safe and watch over him and the other brave soldiers I hold so dear: Jack, Clinton Shaw, John Cartmill, and Jim Stout. I also pray for comfort for their families here at home. Thank you for the good news from Bernice. Please watch over her unborn child and protect Bernice and the baby. And Lord, please ease my suffering too. In Jesus' name."

After that, sleep came.

Daphne sat up, blinked away sleep, but felt no fear. She saw a shadowy figure in her room.

Raymond?

Yes, it was Raymond . . . coming toward her in the darkness, the glint of an unseen light reflecting off his glasses. It was so bright, this light, she had to shield her eyes. *Where was it coming from? Why could she see the brightness, but not the source of it?*

As Raymond approached her, everything else became distant and dim—except his face—his sweet, handsome face. It didn't just reflect the light, it *was* the light, a kind of radiance that seemed to glow from deep within his eyes and even more brilliantly from his smile.

Daphne smiled back at her husband and reached for him, touched him, pulled him close. She breathed deeply, taking in his scent, oh so clean and strong and unmistakable. She ran her fingers over the coarseness of his uniform, ran her fingers beneath the jacket. Felt the beating of his heart. Then, and only then, in the brilliance of the light, did she realize her husband was wearing a different uniform than she had ever seen.

She heard herself utter his name as she reached up to touch his face. But her fingers disappeared in the brilliance and then the brilliance itself vanished, leaving only slivers of streetlight to push through the window blinds and slice the darkness.

Her heart pounded in the silence. It all seemed so real. And yet how could it have been? She had felt his uniform. Curiously, it seemed to be an officer's uniform. But how could that be? For all the times she had dreamt of her husband, for all the times she had seen him and heard his voice in her dreams, she had never been able to touch him and hold him and feel his heart beating in time with hers. Those were the things of reality, not dreams.

Raymond was real, and he had been with her.

But now her arms were empty, emptier than they had ever been.

30

Thursday, September 28, 1944

Daphne decided not to tell anyone of Raymond's visit. After all, how would she explain it? How could she ever hope to make others believe it was real? Still, it filled her mind as the days unfolded and she found herself replaying the whole experience time after time, day after day. The more she did, the more convinced she was that Raymond had been at her bedside. She had felt him . . . held him . . . been comforted by him.

But others wouldn't understand, so she kept it to herself.

Life went on as usual, following the same damnably lonely routine the war had forced upon all of them. Each day was just the same as the one before. Then the Abstons received a telephone call from Clarence. Feeling ill, Bernice had asked her husband to drive her to the local hospital. She miscarried along the way.

31

Sunday, October 1, 1944

The wind whipped around the little Ford Coupe as Daphne drove her parents home from church. Bringing the car to rest in front of the old house, she set the parking brake before turning to her mother sitting beside her. "After lunch, I'm going to visit Bernice to see if she needs help with the house. Would you like to come along, Mother?"

Maggie nodded. "Yes, I would. That sounds like a good idea. I'm sure Bernice could use a little cheering up."

Daphne agreed. She was concerned for her sister, who was still weak and not gaining back her strength as quickly as she should. Though the doctor was still hopeful Bernice could eventually conceive, Daphne knew she still grieved over the loss of yet another baby.

Albert, who had been sitting quietly on the other side of Maggie, spoke up. "Well, ladies I'll ride along too, if you don't mind." So it was settled. They would eat a quick lunch and then head for the Roberts' home.

Just as both car doors slammed shut, their next-door neighbor, Mr. Byroads, hurried over. He looked worried and anxious. Gripped tightly in his hand was a Western Union telegram addressed to Mrs. Raymond Kelley. Daphne grabbed the envelope and tore it open with shaking hands.

THE SECRETARY OF WAR DESIRES ME TO EXPRESS HIS DEEP REGRET THAT YOUR HUSBAND PRIVATE FIRST CLASS RAYMOND R KELLEY HAS BEEN REPORTED MISSING IN ACTION SINCE TEN SEPTEMBER IN FRANCE

IF FURTHER DETAILS OR OTHER INFORMATION ARE RECEIVED YOU WILL BE PROMPTLY NOTIFIED

J. A. ULIO, THE ADJUTANT GENERAL.

Daphne felt the color drain from her face as she looked up at her parents in disbelief. Her father placed one hand on her arm, then with the other hand reached for the telegram. He read it, and then passed it on to his wife. While their neighbor looked on sympathetically, Albert and Maggie gathered their daughter between them and ushered her into the house.

The visit to Bernice put aside, it wasn't long before Reverend Jensen arrived to comfort the family. For the next few hours, Daphne paced aimlessly through the house, her mind unable to settle on a single thought for more than a moment. Was Raymond a prisoner of the Germans? Was he hurt, dying, or lying in some far-off field alone?

As frightened as she was, deep in her heart Daphne held on to the hope he would be found. After all, he had been wounded once before. Surely God wouldn't let anything else happen to him.

When You Come Home

Later that afternoon, Floyd and Twyla dropped by. Soon, the entire Kelley family gathered in the little living room. It was a sober group, as each one quietly anguished in his or her own way. Just what did "Missing in Action" really mean?

Mary slumped on the end of the living room couch, sobbing. Listening to her gut-wrenching cries only deepened Daphne's own distress. It was hard to comfort the young girl when she was in a state of shock herself.

Finally, Leona Kelley drew her daughter aside. "You've got to pull yourself together for Daphne's sake. Don't you think she has enough to handle without having to worry about you?"

Mary swallowed hard and nodded. She turned to her sister-in-law. "Do you think . . . Daphne, could I just . . . could I stay with you tonight?"

"Yes, of course," replied Daphne, sensing they could draw comfort from one another during the oncoming night, which was sure to be a long one. And it was. The girls finally dozed off hours after the household had gone silent.

Mary left mid-morning on Tuesday, and Daphne was kept busy with friends and family who stopped by the house throughout the day. Well-wishers sent flowers. But still, Daphne couldn't remember when she had ever felt so helpless and heartsick or when she had ever gone through such an endlessly long day. Mealtimes were a nauseating challenge as she could barely eat more than a few bites. How could she coax food past the big knot in her throat? She tried reading, but no matter how hard she concentrated, she found herself reading the same page over and over. Her parents tried to console her, but nothing relieved her anxiety.

When Wednesday, October 4th arrived, warm as a summer day but with no further news, Daphne knew she couldn't spend another day cooped up inside. She was ready to escape the confines of the little house and focus on something—anything—other than the news she had received on Sunday.

Deciding to go ahead with the visit to Bernice, Daphne located her pocketbook in the kitchen. Through the window, she caught a glimpse of her father out back. He was leaning against the garden hoe, staring off into space. His flannel shirt sleeves were rolled up, evidence of an unseasonably warm fall day. Daphne walked out the back door and joined him, touching his shoulder to get his attention.

"I'm going to visit Bernice, Dad."

Albert looked down at his daughter as he stood up straight and rubbed his lower back. His eyes were soft with concern.

"Good idea," he said as he glanced down at his muddy work shoes. "I'd come along with you if I was presentable." He rubbed his brow and added, "Have you talked with Raymond's folks yet today?"

"I called Leona and talked a few minutes this morning. But I didn't really know what to say, and I could tell she was at a loss for words too."

"I sure wish I could say something to make you feel better, daughter."

Daphne felt her stomach knot up. "As difficult as it was last spring when Raymond was wounded, this is worse. It's so hard not knowing where he is, if he's being tortured, or somewhere all alone, lost in a strange place, or being held against his will. I can hardly stand it." Daphne stopped. She hadn't intended to share her anguished thoughts with her father. Now, she struggled to hold back the tears, knowing if she released even one, the others would never stay put.

Daphne's father reached out and gently turned her face toward him. "It may seem like there's nothing we can do right now, daughter. But we *can* pray."

Daphne's frustration spilled out. "Oh, Dad, I *have* prayed for Raymond—every single day. And I know others have prayed as well.

Why did God allow this to happen?"

Albert looked dispirited as he stared at his anguished daughter. "I don't know, honey."

"Our prayers haven't kept Raymond safe and they didn't stop Bernice from miscarrying either." Daphne's eyes begged for an answer. "Doesn't God listen?"

Albert looked deep into his daughter's eyes. "Don't for one minute think your prayers are in vain or that they don't matter to God, Daphne. Every prayer is heard and answered, but sometimes not the way we hoped."

Daphne nodded wearily as she reached up and kissed her father's cheek. "I love you, Dad," she said as she dug into her pocketbook for her car keys. "I'd better head out so I can get back before suppertime."

Daphne squeezed her father's arm one last time.

Clarence wasn't home, so she let herself in the front door. Walking into the bedroom, she found Bernice propped up in bed, her pretty face pale and drawn.

"Come here, Daphne, and let me make sure you're all right."

Daphne gently eased herself down on the bed beside Bernice and took her hand. Before her sister could speak, Daphne asked, "How are you feeling, Bernice?"

"I'm really disappointed, but I'll be all right," she replied weakly. "The doctor says I just need to stay off my feet for a while. But what about you, Daphne? I should comfort *you*, you know. Any further word?"

Daphne sighed. "No, and I'm so jumpy I just can't stand it."

"Surely you'll hear something soon." After talking a while longer, Daphne said, "You know, Bernice, I came here to help. What would you like me to do first?"

"Would you mind vacuuming the house?" Daphne patted her hand and, at Bernice's direction, went to the hall closet and took out the sweeper.

Since the house was small, it didn't take Daphne long to finish her task. As she turned off the sweeper, she heard the front door open. Startled, she looked up as her mother walked in, followed hesitantly by Reverend Jensen. His face was tense and much too solemn.

The minister handed Daphne a telegram:

THE SECRETARY OF WAR ASKS THAT I ASSURE YOU OF HIS DEEP SYMPATHY IN THE LOSS OF YOUR HUSBAND PRIVATE FIRST CLASS RAYMOND R KELLEY WHO WAS PREVIOUSLY REPORTED MISSING IN ACTION   REPORT NOW RECEIVED STATES HE WAS KILLED IN ACTION ON TEN SEPTEMBER IN FRANCE LETTER FOLLOWS.

J. A. ULIO, THE ADJUTANT GENERAL.

Daphne's vision blurred and the room became dark. She felt something massive and powerful clamping down on her chest, sucking the air from her lungs. She fell backwards into Clarence's overstuffed chair as the hateful telegram fluttered to the floor.

The next thing Daphne knew, her mother and Bernice had pulled her close, cradling her like a child. Why were they smothering her like this? Didn't they know she couldn't breathe?

She pushed against them and tried to catch her breath, but it burned deep and hot against her heart. She realized her chest was heaving and convulsing and she heard herself sobbing, but she felt nothing. Outside her own body, unable to respond, she hoped she was dead too.

When You Come Home

Raymond, please don't go to heaven without me.

Much later that night, Daphne listlessly changed into her nightgown and walked over to the bedroom window. How had she gotten home? She just couldn't remember. And though it didn't really matter, she felt bewildered at not knowing.

Outside, the darkness matched her loneliness. For the first time since receiving the news, she was alone with her thoughts. She couldn't accept that Raymond would never be coming back. Ever since his departure for basic training nearly two years before, she had never allowed herself to grasp such a ridiculous notion. How could she believe it now? How could it be true?

Oh Raymond, I need you. Please don't leave me. Oh, Raymond . . .

Deep into the night and unable to sleep, Daphne's thoughts remained elusive and without form. Where was God's comfort now that she needed it most? Where was His peace? Why was there only anguish, despair, and unquenchable grief?

She dropped to her knees before the dresser, but before she could form the words of another prayer, she doubled over and wept uncontrollably.

The slivers of light sliced the darkness again, and now they stabbed her with unrelenting force.

WHEN SKIES ARE GRAY

32

Sunday, October 8, 1944

So many cards. So many flowers.

So many visitors, and still they came. Family and friends meant well, but often they intruded on Daphne's deep and private anguish. Somehow she knew eventually she would appreciate their caring. But all she really wanted now was to be left alone to mourn for Raymond.

"She's sleeping right now," Daphne heard her mother say into the phone, though she suspected Maggie knew better. Daphne turned to look at the clock, but for some reason it was turned away from her. Why was that? Oh yes, now she remembered. She had hidden its face because the hands seemed to be moving much too slowly, making her heartbroken insomnia all the worse. But she didn't need to see the clock to know at that very moment the Milledgeville Methodist Church was holding a dual memorial service for Raymond and another church member/soldier who had been killed overseas. The other Kelleys would be there, but Daphne had chosen not to attend. Her grief was still too raw.

She got up from the bed and walked to her dresser to turn the clock back around, but instead, she was distracted by the new gold star lying on top of the dresser. She had her father purchase it the day before, more from a sense of duty than pride. How had she ever thought the stars beautiful?

Ceremoniously, but not without bitterness, she removed the silver star from her window and replaced it with gold. It was the public proclamation of her loss and it made her sick.

As she stood before the window absently twisting her wedding ring, the scenes beyond the glass blurred and were replaced in her mind by images of her brief time with Raymond. Lemonade, candy necklaces, and snuggies appeared before her. She pictured again their windy wedding day and those carefree days when she followed her husband around the states while he trained to be a soldier. She pictured him in his uniform, the uniform he wore when she had held him close time after time; the uniform he had been wearing as he came to her in the night just a month earlier. Was it a dream or a vision? Whatever it was still troubled her. And yet, strangely, it comforted her. From now on, she decided, she would say it was a visit. He came to tell her goodbye.

But so quickly the visit had ended and Raymond was gone. She couldn't believe how naïve she had been. Her biggest concern had always been how to cope with the long separations, but it had never occurred to her the separation might be forever.

By the time Monday came around, Daphne knew the grief would consume her if she gave in to it. To keep that from happening, she decided to keep her appointment with the dentist to have her remaining two wisdom teeth pulled. Truth was, she hoped the pain in her mouth would help her forget the ache in her heart. Instead, it compounded her troubles. In her weakened physical state, the medication administered in the examination room caused a light-headedness that nearly made her faint right in the dental chair.

That afternoon while Daphne was recovering, Ruth and Earl came to visit. Daphne had been dozing and woke to find Ruth sitting next to her in bed, gently rubbing her shoulder.

"How long have you been here?" Daphne murmured, forcing herself to sit up.

Ruth glanced at her wristwatch. "A couple of hours."

"Why didn't you wake me?" Daphne's mouth was so dry she could barely form words.

Ruth picked up the bottle of pain killers from the bedside table. "Because Mother said you had taken one of these and we should probably let you sleep for a while. Are you feeling any better?"

"I don't know . . . I'm all right, I guess."

"Well, you're *not* all right. Dad said you almost fainted at the dentist's office this morning. Why in the world didn't you postpone your appointment for a while?" Ruth admonished her younger sister. "Were your teeth bothering you that much?"

"Yes." Daphne closed her eyes for a minute and shook her head wearily in confusion. "Well, no. Oh, I don't know. I just wanted to get it over with." She touched her cheek and grimaced. "The pain medicine seems to be wearing off."

"Just lay back, honey. I'll get a cold rag for your jaw."

Daphne positioned her pillow behind her head and rubbed the sleep from her eyes. Her mouth felt like it was full of cotton.

Ruth returned and Daphne took several swallows of cold water before setting the tumbler on the table. Ruth folded the wet, cool washcloth and held it out to Daphne. "Let's see if this helps."

Daphne cradled the icy cloth against her warm cheek. "Oh, that's nice."

Maggie appeared in the doorway. "Daphne, why don't you take another pain pill?"

"I think I should wait until bedtime. I don't want to be too drowsy to eat supper and I need something in my stomach for the medicine."

"You're right," Maggie replied. "You do need to eat."

"Haven't you been eating like you should?" Ruth's face registered concern as she looked her little sister up and down.

"Sort of. But it's hard to eat when you have no appetite."

Maggie walked further into the room. "We're having vegetable soup and Aunt Ellie's oatmeal bread for supper. You'd better eat *something* or you'll waste away."

Daphne didn't promise. She didn't care.

"Did I hear something about supper?" Earl stood in the doorway and looked at his sister-in-law. "Are these ladies bothering you, Daphne?"

Daphne gave him a weak half-smile. "They're trying to make me fat, Earl."

"Well, you look fine to me."

"You're nice, Earl." Daphne mumbled as she rested her head against the pillow.

Ruth squeezed her sister's arm. "Now, don't go back to sleep, Daphne. Is your pain any better?"

Daphne opened an eye and gently rubbed her jaw. It did feel better. In fact, *she* felt better. Just having Ruth and Earl here cheered her up. She threw aside the towel and slowly stood up. "That compress seems to have helped. Let's go get supper ready for your starving husband, Ruth."

Ruth grinned. "Thatta girl." She steadied her sister and together they followed Maggie and Earl into the kitchen.

Every spoonful of the delicious vegetable soup was hot and soothing. Daphne managed to eat enough to satisfy the watchful eyes of her family. She swallowed another pain pill with her last sip of water. She helped her mother and Ruth wash and dry the dishes, listening to their conversation, but joining in only when questioned. As the medication took hold, the pain lessened and Daphne's eyes began to droop.

Ruth seemed to notice. "Come on, Daphne. Let's get you ready for bed." Back in the bedroom, she helped Daphne into her night clothes and tucked her into bed.

"You're treating me just like a baby," Daphne protested sleepily.

"That's all right, honey." Ruth gave her little sister a hug. "You get some sleep now."

Daphne rolled onto her side and was asleep by the time Ruth turned out the light.

The next afternoon, Ruth said, "Daphne, why don't you come home with us for a few weeks?"

Albert looked over at his youngest daughter. "That's a good idea. Daphne, why *don't* you go with your sister? It'll do you good to get away from here for a while."

So, the next day Daphne packed a few outfits, climbed into the back seat of the Humphreys' dust-covered Plymouth and headed for the backwoods of central Illinois.

The Humphreys' house backed up to a small thicket. Down a steep embankment flowed a brook surrounded by more trees. The fall weather had turned the property into a collage of crimson, orange, and yellow. The view from the house was an unframed work of art by the Creator.

At the old farmhouse, Daphne found comfort in the quiet, sometimes taking long solitary walks and meandering with Ruth down the nearly deserted country road. Each night she prayed for strength and courage to face the coming day. But deeper inside, she wanted answers. Raymond had been a good Christian man. His warm personality, along with his extensive knowledge of the scriptures, would have served him well in the ministry. So why wasn't he given the opportunity to become the Reverend "Deed" Kelley? Why would God let such a good man die?

Why did God let *her* good man die?

One afternoon, as Daphne walked alone down the country road, she approached the point at which she always turned around and headed back to Ruth and Earl's house. But as she turned, an unwelcome, ear-shattering noise came from the woods. A gunshot! Instantly, Daphne dropped to her knees, defenseless and small, bowing to the sound of war.

As the echo of the gunshot faded, Daphne was surprised to find she resented even the hunter who was responsible for the same sound that had taken Raymond from her. She was overcome by the realization Raymond must have been frightened every moment of every day. Yet he had protected her and kept her from knowing his terror.

Daphne felt new tears rising, but these tears crested on the wave of an anguished wail from deep inside her very soul. She felt her empty arms reaching for the sky—reaching up to God.

"When will it stop?" she cried. "Hasn't there already been enough killing?"

She tried to clear her eyes as she confronted the slow moving clouds. "Lord, why did Raymond have to die? Why couldn't he come home to me?"

The young widow held her head in her hands, continuing her desperate prayer vigil until a burst of sunlight came through the clouds. She had the strangest feeling she was being watched. As she lifted her head and strained to see through the tears, something moved in the brush and caught her eye. Raising her hand to shield the sun, Daphne located the hunter's prey darting near the edge of the clearing. The young deer was so frightened it pranced in a bewildered, aimless gait. But when the animal saw her, it stopped for just a second and stared intently at her before bolting back into the woods.

Daphne shuddered, certain the little fawn had chosen a deadly path. But then it reappeared, taking tentative steps toward her until it stood exposed in the bright sunlight.

"It looks just like the deer Raymond sketched on the V-Mail card after he was wounded," Daphne whispered to herself. For the longest time, girl and fawn studied each other—not moving, barely breathing. Only when a cloud again blanketed the sun did the deer disappear into the brush. Daphne struggled to say a prayer for safety even as she listened expectantly for another gunshot which never came.

As she listened, a verse from Psalm 42 ran through her head: *As the deer pants for streams of water, so my soul pants for you, O God.* Daphne thought about the words. Just as the fragile little deer depended upon water to survive, she knew that she, too, must rely upon God to meet her spiritual needs. Since Raymond's death, she hadn't done that. By allowing her anger to build, she had distanced herself from the Lord. Now, God's gentle message seemed as clear as if spoken out loud:

Depend upon Me.

A month ago, the Lord had allowed her an amazing visit from Raymond, and today He had touched a drawing and made it come alive.

What further proof did she need that God loved her and cared about her? She closed her eyes, submitting to His comforting arms.

This was day one of her spiritual recovery.

33

November, 1944

Winter crept ever so slowly into central Indiana. Though she wasn't looking forward to facing the public yet, Daphne realized she couldn't put off returning to the beauty shop forever.

"I'm going back to work today," Daphne announced early one chilly Wednesday morning as she walked into the kitchen and reached for the coffee pot.

Albert was sitting at the kitchen table reading the morning newspaper. When he looked up, his face held encouragement. "I think that's a good idea, Daphne. Getting out of the house and busying yourself with your customers and friends will be good medicine."

Maggie closed the ice box door. "Are you sure you're ready, Daphne? What about the long hours your boss requires you girls to work?"

Daphne poured a cup of coffee and added some sugar before taking a sip. "I talked with Vera a few days ago and she said I can ease back into my work schedule a day at a time. She hasn't pushed me to return, but I know my absence has placed a burden on the other girls." Her words held certainty. "It's time I went back."

Daphne was welcomed back with gentle hugs from Mrs. Shook and the other beauticians. She was grateful for their kindness, including the way they all tried to avoid discussing the war.

It took effort on her part, but Daphne kept the conversations with her customers focused on the trivial and home front things like movies, music, and which downtown shops were opening or closing.

There was no reason to look forward to the daily mail delivery; it was now just a hurtful reminder of happier days. Even the postman seemed sensitive to her feelings. He no longer whistled or teased her like before. Instead, he quietly opened the front door, sometimes wincing at the squealing of the hinges and the sound of the cowbell as he slipped the mail onto an empty chair. Sadness shadowed his kind face. It was obvious he wished he didn't have to deliver the unopened letters Daphne had mailed to Raymond.

And then, toward the middle of November, one last envelope from her beloved soldier arrived. Hands shaking, Daphne carried the envelope to the back room and placed it in her pocketbook. All day long, her stomach clenched with anxiety as she considered what might be in the letter.

It wasn't until late that night, long after the house was dark and quiet that Daphne found the courage to open the envelope. It was a short letter.

Dearest Daphne,

Please forgive the brevity of this letter, sweetheart, but I wanted to quickly share some good news. I'm to be promoted to staff sergeant. I guess that means I'm doing what they expect of me, so I'm honored and humbled. Of course, I always expect more of myself, and I fear that I might always fall short of my aim to do more and to be the best I can be. When I come home, darling, I know I will want to be a better husband to you than I am capable of being. Know this; both you and the Lord inspire me to do good things and to be a good man. You are forever my sunshine. I love you.

Raymond

Though the days were long, the nights were longer. Sleep always came slowly and when Daphne finally did doze off, she slept fitfully. Although she had completely recovered from her oral surgery, her appetite had not improved much and she still had to force herself to eat. Her weight dropped to eighty-four pounds, prompting customer comments and the suggestion that she see a doctor. After a thorough examination, the doctor announced her immune system needed strengthening and prescribed weekly iron shots. She disliked needles, but dutifully submitted to the weekly injections.

The Kelleys were not faring much better. It saddened Daphne to see the sorrow on the faces of Guy and Leona. And poor Mary. She was having such a difficult time coping with the loss of her big brother.

With the passing days and reflection on Raymond's nighttime appearance nearly two months before, Daphne's anger continued to dissolve. She knew—and had always known, really—that it wasn't God's will for Raymond to die. It was God's will that Raymond receive the call to "victory," a call Raymond most assuredly answered with unbounded joy. She found solace in what it said in I Corinthians, *Death is swallowed up in victory...* and that this victory comes *through our Lord Jesus Christ.*

When You Come Home

Yes, certainly God grieved with her, just as surely as He gave her strength through His ever-present love. In fact, evidence of His love was all around her: in her family who mourned with her, in her friends who cared enough to send almost two hundred cards of concern and encouragement, and in the Bible passages that spoke directly to her. She turned to her Bible often. One of her favorite scriptures was Psalm 121, where she found comfort in the words:

I will lift up mine eyes unto the hills, from whence cometh my help.

My help cometh from the LORD, which made heaven and earth.

He will not suffer thy foot to be moved: he that keepeth thee will not slumber.

Behold, he that keepeth Israel shall neither slumber nor sleep.

The LORD is thy keeper: the LORD is thy shade upon thy right hand.

The sun shall not smite thee by day, nor the moon by night.

The LORD shall preserve thee from all evil: he shall preserve thy soul.

The LORD shall preserve thy going out and thy coming in from this time forth, and even for evermore.

Despite her recovering faith, it still took every ounce of Daphne's determination to go forward. And though she worked hard to maintain her composure, at times she knew her suffering showed. Her parents tried to reach out to her but seeing her own sorrow reflected in their eyes, she tried to be brave. How could she add to their misery? After all, both of them had grown to love Raymond as a son and they, too, were devastated by his death. Not until she was alone at night, curled up in her big bed, could she really give in to the grief she held at bay during the daylight hours.

As the days dragged on, Daphne half-heartedly listened to the war news flooding the airwaves. It was reported that U.S. troops had begun bombing Japan, and the Allies were attacking Germany by air. U.S. bombers were hitting targets by day and the British were bombing by night.

Still more soldiers were at risk each day. They were sons and brothers and fathers. They were husbands.

And they were dying.

34

End of November, 1944

"Did you hear about the beauty shop for sale here in town, Daphne?" May was meticulously sweeping up piles of hair in her booth area as she glanced over at Daphne.

Daphne lay down her scissors. Before replying, she ran her fingers through Mrs. Jenkins' curly dark blonde hair, measuring for symmetry. "No, I didn't. Where is it?"

"In the Heflin building, on the corner of Meridian and Main."

Daphne nodded. "I know where it is. The LeMar Shop is in that building." Daphne snipped at a few more strands of hair. "How did you find out about it?"

"Annabelle mentioned it at lunch yesterday. I guess she saw an ad in *The Lebanon Reporter*."

"Telephone call for you, May," Lera Shook's voice rang out. May propped the broom against the wall and reached for the phone, ending the conversation.

Daphne was intrigued. The rest of the day as she tended to her customers, she thought about what it would be like to operate her very own salon. She had entertained such thoughts before, but never seriously. So much of her time had been devoted to her life with Raymond. But now, it was a possibility.

The next day Daphne scheduled her customers around a late lunch so she could eat alone. It was close to two o'clock when she folded up her napkin at Wheeler's Restaurant and took the last sip of coffee. As she reached for her pocketbook, restaurant owner Charlie Wheeler leaned over the polished black countertop and eyed her plate. "You didn't eat much, little lady. Was anything wrong?"

Chagrined because her wastefulness had been noticed, Daphne quickly reassured him. "No, no. Everything was fine. I just wasn't very hungry." Pulling a ticket pad from his pocket, Charlie nodded kindly. "Surely you've got room for a slice of Mom's butterscotch pie, Daphne. It just came out of the oven."

Daphne sat quietly. Though she tried to eat enough to provide adequate nourishment, mealtimes continued to be a challenge. Would she ever again really enjoy the pies and cakes Sara Jane Wheeler was famous for? She sighed. "I'm sorry, Charlie. Not today." After counting out thirty cents for the sandwich and plunking down a nickel for the coffee, Daphne pulled on her coat and gloves and left the restaurant. Walking briskly, she crossed town and reached the east side a few minutes later.

Daphne stopped in front of the tall stone building and peered through the wide plate glass window. Taped to the bottom right-hand corner was a poster advertising the purchase of war bonds. It cleverly depicted one of Norman Rockwell's paintings titled, *Save Freedom of Worship*. She momentarily closed her eyes and quietly protested, "But Lord, why does freedom have to come at such a high price?" Before her misery could take hold, Daphne opened the door and walked into the spacious lobby. Looking around, she noticed several doors with frosted windows and a flight of stairs straight ahead against the far wall. No one was around, so she walked across the room and climbed the steps to the second story. The salon was at the top of the stairs. Surprised to find it unlocked, Daphne turned the knob and entered the vacant suite. There were two rooms: a shampoo and work room with space for two or three operators, and a reception area. The layout was workable, she thought. With a few minor improvements, she felt the place would be more than adequate. And she certainly liked the location. Across from the courthouse, attracting downtown shoppers was definitely a possibility.

Walking back to the Ione Beauty Shop, Daphne considered her future now that she was faced with being alone. She realized operating her own business would be demanding, but it could also provide more security and a better income for the coming years. The more she had to occupy her mind, the better.

She decided to make an offer on the shop, but first wanted her father's approval. That night after supper was over and the dishes washed and dried, she approached him. He was sitting in his chair, eyes half closed, just about to doze off. She touched his arm gently.

"Dad?"

"Hmmm?" Albert's eyes slowly opened wider. "What's the matter, Daphne?"

Daphne sat down on the floor at her father's feet. "You know I've always said someday I'd like to own my own beauty shop?"

Albert sat up straighter in his chair and eyed his daughter thoughtfully. He smiled. "Uh-huh, I reckon you've said something about that quite a few times."

"Well, I've found a place for sale here in Lebanon. It's a suite of rooms in the Heflin building on the corner of Meridian and Main Street. I went there today and looked it over. It's really a nice place and I think it would be the perfect location for a salon." Daphne paused and fortified herself with a deep breath. "Of course, I'd need to take out a loan to get started."

Albert's fingers drummed against the crocheted arm rests of the chair as his eyes narrowed in thought. "Is this place already set up for a beauty shop?"

"Yes it is. There's space for what I need, and enough extra room to add one or maybe two more operators later on." Daphne looked intently at her father, silently willing him to understand. "I think this is what I want to do, Dad."

Daphne watched concern cloud her father's eyes.

"Honey, I'm not sure borrowing money right now is wise. We're in the middle of a war, for goodness sake."

Knowing her father had borrowed heavily during the depression and lost his farm because of it, Daphne was prepared for his reaction. "I know it's a big undertaking, Dad, but I've been giving this a lot of thought and I really think I can make a success of it. And as far as the financing goes, would you consider letting me borrow the money Jack's been sending you and Mother?"

Her father's brow creased as he considered her request, then softened as he said, "I don't see why not."

Once the financing was secured, it didn't take long to complete the necessary paperwork. By the first of December, the little shop was officially hers.

The name was perfect: The Daphne-Ray Beauty Salon.

When You Come Home

35

Christmas Eve, 1944

It was nearly midnight and the Abston home was dark and still, except for the radio in Daphne's room playing soft Christmas music. It had been a wet, dreary day, but as night fell and the temperature dropped, the rain changed to snow. Dressed in flannel pajamas, Daphne stood at her bedroom window taking in the night scene, noticing how the glistening white snow brightened the street as the flakes fluttered down and covered the sidewalks and rooftops.

It was beautiful. But it was terrible. How could it be so quiet and peaceful when there was fighting, maiming, and killing going on overseas? How could she be safe and warm when soldiers were freezing and lonely and craving sleep in their foxholes?

As tears once again filled her eyes, tender memories of Raymond filled her heart, but even the happy thoughts carried with them an almost unbearable anguish and longing. If only she could feel his strong arms holding her just one more time. Oh, there were so many "if onlys." *If only* Raymond hadn't been separated from his original group—*if only* he had been sent home after he was injured the first time—*if only* there had been more time for them to be together as man and wife.

On the radio, Daphne heard the sounds of *I'll be Home for Christmas.* As she listened to the words of the beautiful song, she knew her soldier wouldn't be home for Christmas now or ever again. Tears streamed down her face as she rose from the window, walked over to the radio and sadly turned the knob.

In the darkness she felt her way back to her empty bed.

Oh Raymond, I wish you were here.

Christmas morning dawned cold, but clear and bright. The snow that had fallen so heavily during the night had diminished to a few wispy flakes which seemed to be nothing more than an afterthought from the heavens. The scene outside the window was an artist's dream: houses, cars, mailboxes, and sidewalks all covered with a thick white blanket glistening in the morning sun. Inside the warm little kitchen, Daphne and her mother worked side-by-side preparing Christmas dinner. Soon the aroma of mincemeat pie and homemade rolls drifted through the house.

Resting comfortably in his favorite living room chair, Albert's eyes were closed as he listened to the latest war news on the radio. Daphne glanced through the doorway. Her father looked so sad. She knew his heart was heavy, not only for her but also for the thousands of Americans dying overseas, their families back home, and for all the victims of the long war.

A loud knock brought the retired minister to his feet. Daphne wiped her hands on her apron and joined him as he pulled open the door to welcome Bernice and Clarence. Laden with presents, they rushed into the warm house, stomping the snow off their boots.

When You Come Home

"Hello and Merry Christmas!" announced Clarence with gusto.

"Merry Christmas," replied Daphne and her father in unison. Daphne embraced her sister and patted her brother-in-law's arm. "Here, let me take your coats."

Bernice stuck her head into the kitchen. "I'll be in to help you in just a minute, Mother." She followed Daphne into the bedroom and helped her spread the coats out on the bed. Slipping her arm around her little sister, Bernice looked intently into Daphne's eyes. "Are you all right, honey?"

"Yes." But Daphne knew her face betrayed her. "I'm glad you and Clarence were able to come, especially with the snow and all. Families should be together at Christmas."

Bernice nodded and gave Daphne another squeeze as they returned to the living room in time to hear Albert questioning Clarence, "How are the roads?"

"They're getting slick, especially at the intersections," Clarence said. "But there's certainly not enough snow to keep us home on Christmas day."

"Well, I hope Ruth and Earl won't have any trouble getting here," said Albert with a worried tone. "They have a long way to come."

Daphne reassured her father. "Now, Dad, you know Earl is a careful driver. I'm sure they'll be fine."

Less than an hour later, the Humphreys pulled into the driveway. Into the warm house they trudged, dragging boxes of colorful packages and more snow. Daughter and son-in-law embraced Maggie and Albert, then gave Daphne a warm hug as they studied her closely. She forced a smile to assure them she was all right. It was good to have her family surrounding her.

The women returned to the kitchen to assist with the meal

preparations. Soon a dinner of ham, sweet potatoes, homemade rolls, greens beans, and cranberry salad, along with Maggie's homemade mincemeat pie was set upon the table. As the family enjoyed Christmas dinner, they talked and laughed, carefully avoiding any mention of the war. Knowing their concern about her weight loss, Daphne added more second helpings to her plate than she really wanted. She smiled absently, pretending to be joyful in order to not infect others with her despair. But when the evening was over, Daphne was relieved. As she fell into bed, her holiday smile disappeared for the rest of the season.

36

January, 1945

The Daphne-Ray Beauty Salon officially opened for business on a bitter cold January 2, 1945. Daphne didn't take her role as business owner lightly. In beauty school, instructors had emphasized the importance of treating every customer with the utmost courtesy and respect. And now the young beautician was determined her shop would reflect those high standards. She invested considerable time in choosing top-notch equipment and quality beauty supplies, while carefully comparing prices. She desperately wanted her business to succeed, and she *needed* it to succeed.

All in all, Daphne was pleased with the flow of customers and positive comments received as the small business took root. She found the overall demands of managing the shop, combined with her hair-styling appointments, a blessing in keeping her mind off the emptiness in her heart. Each month she planned to repay part of the money she had borrowed from Jack's account. By her calculations, she should be debt-free within the year, she thought with satisfaction.

But as busy as she was, there were many times when some unexpected incident would bring her to the brink of despair. One morning on her way to work, a customer, Elberta Throckgilder, reached out and stopped her on the sidewalk. After offering her sympathy, the woman added, "Aren't you glad you visited your soldier so often while you could?"

Daphne couldn't believe her ears and struggled to hide her anger, for this was the same woman who had chastised her and other Army wives for chasing their husbands "all over the country." Daphne simply swallowed her disgust and continued on.

But it wasn't just the unwittingly cruel comments of others that affected her. Sometimes it was just the glimpse of a man in uniform or perhaps a wayward scent of Raymond's familiar aftershave. Sometimes in the midst of a hectic day, she caught herself staring into space and thinking of Raymond's blue eyes, or watching a reflection in a window and remembering how he had repeatedly walked by the salon before asking her out for the first time. Just the day before, she had awakened in the middle of the night to the sound of footsteps. She had bolted upright in bed, certain Raymond was coming to see her again, only to realize the footsteps were her father's as he headed to the kitchen for a drink of water.

Memories Daphne had once called upon to sustain her while she waited for Raymond's return now threatened her sanity. Too many phrases and catchy jingles reminded her of her husband. *You Are My Sunshine* maintained its popularity across the country. One afternoon as the song came on the radio, Daphne nearly fell as she tripped over her own feet hurrying to change the station. No one could ever sing that song the way Raymond did and she despaired at knowing never again would she receive a letter ending with *P.S. You Are My Sunshine.*

37

February, 1945

The distant sun had long since set as Mary Francis Parrish Mohr came through the door of the Daphne-Ray Beauty Salon after trudging through ice and sludge. Daphne was rather surprised to see the young beautician so late in the evening, but she was between customers and glad for the chance to visit. She had heard Mary Francis was residing with her parents while her husband, Forrest, was overseas fighting, and wondered how the young woman was coping. Daphne remembered Forrest as a nice-looking man with brown curly hair. He was a barber, and he used to walk by the beauty shop on his way to work. Daphne hung up her friend's coat and invited Mary Francis to sit down.

"Have you heard from Forrest lately?" Daphne inquired as she swept the floor around the styling chair.

"Not for a week or two," Mary Francis said. "He's on the front, you know, so I don't get many letters." Her voice trailed off and her eyes took on a faraway look. "I guess you know how that goes."

Daphne put away her broom and sat down to face Mary Francis. After a few moments of silence, Mary Francis took a deep breath and continued, "Daphne, the reason I'm here is because, well . . . I'd like to know if you have any room for me in your shop."

Daphne was taken by surprise. She had actually purchased the shop thinking some day she would expand and include more operators. She just hadn't thought the time would come so soon, or that someone with Mary Francis' following and experience would make her an offer.

The shop *had* been a bit lonely, even with the steady stream of customers. At the Ione, there had been plenty of opportunities to chat with her co-workers between customers. Daphne missed the camaraderie. It would be comforting to have an understanding, familiar face in the salon. She made this important business decision with pleasure and confidence.

"Mary Francis, I think it sounds like a wonderful idea. It won't take long to set up your booth. When can you begin?"

Mary Francis' brown eyes lit up with delight. "Oh, I could probably be ready around the end of February."

So it was settled. In two weeks, young war bride Mary Francis would join the Daphne-Ray Salon.

Later that week, Daphne received a letter from Raymond's buddy, Private First Class William Hicks.

Mrs. Kelley,

Raymond was one of my very best friends. I think perhaps he spoke of me in some of his letters to you. I knew him to be an honest and fearless soldier, a true comrade and friend, and a most faithful husband.

When You Come Home

He was very conscientious in everything he did and was well liked by all the officers and enlisted men in our company.

Please allow me to share your great sorrow. Your loss was also my loss, though not so great. Rest assured that you can be as proud of him in death as you were in life. He died a true hero's death—fighting for his country, his loved ones, and the things we all hold dear.

My deepest sympathy to you and all his loved ones.

Sincerely yours,
Pfc. William H. Hicks

Daphne blinked away tears as she folded the pages back together. Though grateful for the young man's kind and eloquent words, they resurrected questions she couldn't shrug off. How did Raymond die? Did he die instantly? Was it a sudden attack? Did the enemy take his body? What were his final hours like?

Later that night, she wrote William Hicks, hoping for answers. Never in her life had a letter been so difficult to write and her stomach twisted with each word.

I might hate what I find out, she thought, *but I have to know.*

38

March 27, 1945

Nearly a month had passed since Mary Francis had been hired, and Daphne thanked God for nudging the woman in her direction. Her friend proved to be a skilled hairdresser with a willingness to work hard and put in long hours. Business was brisk. In fact, things were going so well Daphne decided it was time to expand even further. In the last week, she had added Barbara Tanselle, a young woman fresh out of beauty school, to work Tuesdays, Thursdays, and Saturdays. Once the young beautician developed a following, Daphne planned to increase her hours. Nearly every day the salon was filled with the sounds of murmured feminine conversations and the soothing hum of hair dryers.

Usually, Daphne brought a sandwich for lunch and stayed in the shop to eat, but since it was Tuesday, the special at Wheeler's Restaurant was fried chicken, one of her favorites. Mary Francis and Barbara had scheduled customers through their lunch hour so Daphne had to eat out alone. Now, as she walked back to the shop, she slowed her pace, enjoying the unseasonably warm and breezy spring day. When she reached the Heflin building, she opened the door, hurried up the stairs, and entered the Daphne-Ray Salon. Barbara rushed to her, pale and anxious as she cried, "Oh Daphne, thank goodness you're back. Things are a mess here. Mary Francis just got a telegram that Forrest is missing in action!"

Daphne's eyes widened in disbelief. "Oh, no."

"Oh, yes!" Clearly the young girl was beginning to panic so Daphne put an arm around her, hoping to calm her. There were three customers in the shop, two under the dryers and one in the styling chair. They all looked stunned.

Daphne led Barbara to the back of the room, put her hands on the younger girl's shoulders and said softly, "Now tell me exactly what happened."

Barbara drew a deep breath. "About half an hour ago, some man in uniform came into the shop and asked for Mary Francis. When she came forward, he handed her the telegram. She read it and burst into tears. Then she grabbed her coat and headed for the door. On her way out, she said something like, 'Tell Daphne I'm sorry, but I just can't stay.'"

Daphne's heart broke as she silently prayed Mary Francis had not been dealt the devastating blow she herself had suffered.

"What will we do with her customers, Daphne?"

Daphne pulled herself back to the present. "I'll finish them. You work on your own customers for now, but if you have extra time later on, let me know."

For the rest of the day Daphne somberly, yet professionally, threw herself into serving both her customers and Mary Francis's customers. Her hands flew as she wrapped pin curl after pin curl. It was well past dark when the last customer walked out the door. Feet weary and hands cramping, Daphne displayed the now welcome "Closed" sign in the front window, locked the shop, and slowly walked down the stairs and out the lobby door. Hunching her shoulders against the now chilly wind, she headed to her car for the short drive to the Parrish residence.

Once inside the too-quiet house, Daphne sat down with Mary Francis, comforting her as best she could, advising her to take some time off work and promising to take care of her customers while she was away. As she bundled up for the drive home, her thoughts again focused on the war. Until now, such thoughts had made her angry. But today she was just tired of it all, worn out by the endless fighting and killing.

Two long days passed with no word from Mary Francis. A sick feeling settled in Daphne's stomach and she decided to check up on her friend. After closing and locking the door of the little salon, she headed once again for the Parrish residence. Parking her car on a side street, she walked briskly up to the large, two-story house and pressed the buzzer at the front door.

Mrs. Parrish greeted her. "Well hello, Daphne, come in and get out of the cold." Pointing toward the other room, the older woman lowered her voice. "She'll be glad to see you, I know. I'll get you girls some hot coffee while the two of you visit."

As soon as Daphne entered the living room, Mary Francis rose from the davenport. Her eyes filled with welling tears as she accepted Daphne's warm embrace. "Thank you so much for taking my customers, Daphne. I didn't intend to leave you in the lurch, but I just had to get away."

Daphne tugged off her heavy gloves. "You don't have to explain, Mary Francis. I know what you're going through."

When You Come Home

Mary Francis's face took on a determined look. "But I am going to return to work tomorrow."

Daphne nodded. "We'll be glad to have you back. We sure miss you."

A sharp knock on the front door interrupted the conversation. Mary Francis looked surprised. Hesitantly she walked across the room and pulled the heavy door open. There stood a Red Cross volunteer, and to Daphne's horror, in his hand was a familiar-looking telegram. Mary Francis grew pale as she looked up at the dreaded messenger. Daphne's eyes remained on the volunteer as Mary Francis took the telegram from him. How many death notices had this man already given out, she wondered?

And how many more were still to come?

39

Spring, 1945

As budding trees sprouted leaves and the grass thickened and turned green, Daphne felt her spirits rise. Flowers were springing up all over and her father's roses were in bloom, adding a splash of vibrant color to the little house on Green Street.

Mary Francis seemed to be coping well with her husband's death, at least on the surface. Like Daphne, she worked long hours at the shop in a vain attempt to stave off the loneliness and despair that awaited during the endless evenings. Neither woman wished to call attention to her own grief, for they were just two of the thousands who had lost husbands, sons, or fathers. They were only two of the countless survivors who were, themselves, victims. Daphne wasn't quite sure if it was a particularly cruel twist of fate that had placed the two war widows in one small beauty salon, or if it was a blessing they had each other to lean on.

Once the warmth of spring crept back into the air, Frances Kelley and her friend Betty Baldwin stopped by the shop several times a week on their way home from school. At thirteen, Frances was as lively as ever and blossoming into a pretty young lady. Raymond would have been surprised at how quickly his little sister was growing up, Daphne thought. And as soon as the thought entered her mind, she realized she was starting to think of Raymond in the past tense. Raymond *would have been* surprised by Frances—he *would have been* saddened to see Mary Kelley so distraught—he *would have been* a great consoler for Mary Francis—he *would have been* pleased to learn his friend Jim Gates had been spared from military service as the only son to tend the family farm, and that he and Mamie were blessed with a baby boy of their own on March 1st.

It was Saturday afternoon and Daphne kept one eye on the clock as she brushed Mary Kelley's hair. Pauline Cartmill was stopping by the shop for a quick visit and Daphne was looking forward to seeing her.

"What time is your friend due to arrive, Daphne?"

"Around three o'clock, but I hope she gets here earlier so you can meet her." Daphne parted off a small section of Mary's dark brown hair. "Are we just doing a trim?"

Mary nodded. "It needs to stay long so I can roll it up in back to keep it away from the machinery at work."

"What's new at Winklers?"

"We're busier than ever producing shells for the war. Did you hear that we recently produced our two-millionth 81-MM mortar shell? The story made the Lebanon *and* Indianapolis papers. Now we've opened a second line to double production on that shell."

Daphne put down her scissors. "My, that *is* big news. I'm sure you're proud to be a part of the production crew behind the accomplishment.

Are you still in the company choir?"

Mary nodded. "Yes. We've got around twenty women singing now, and it's so much fun."

"Who are some of the girls?"

Mary paused to think. "Let's see, there's Rosaline Franklin. I don't really know her too well, but she has a beautiful voice. Corinne Pulliam Quayle is in the group. She's really nice. You've probably heard of the Pulliam family."

Daphne nodded. "I know they own *The Lebanon Reporter* as well as several other papers in Indiana."

"That's right. Then there's Sue Ulen Shera."

"Isn't she related to Henry Ulen who built the Ulen County Club in town?"

"Yes, she is. And I'm thrilled we've been asked to sing there next week."

"Don't forget to tell me how that goes. I heard your choir at First Baptist last year and the presentation was excellent."

Mary smiled. "Thank you, Daphne."

Daphne brushed wisps of hair off the styling cape covering Mary's shoulders. "By the way, do you ever hear from your friend, Bud Sedwick?"

"Yes. We write back and forth nearly every week, but he doesn't say much."

"Is he still fighting in the Philippines?"

Mary nodded somberly. "Yes. I'll be so glad when he comes home."

Judging by the look on her sister-in-law's face, Mary had developed deep feelings for the young soldier. Daphne prayed the Lord would send him back home safely. "Why don't you come to church with me on Sunday and stay for dinner? Mother bought a nice roast yesterday and it's too big for just the three of us."

Mary's face brightened. "I'd love to, Daphne."

"Good. We'll look forward to it." As Daphne eased the styling chair down with her foot, the front door opened. "Well, here's Pauline now." Daphne hurried over to welcome her friend.

Pauline Cartmill's greeting was warm. "Hello Daphne. It's wonderful to see you." As Daphne walked into her friend's embrace, she felt her throat tighten. The last time she had seen Pauline, Raymond had been beside her.

Stepping back, Daphne cleared her throat before introducing Pauline to Mary Kelley, and to Mary Francis Mohr, who had slipped in behind Pauline. The women chatted for a few minutes, then Mary left for home and Mary Francis headed to the back of the room to eat a sandwich.

Daphne circled the shop's two rooms with Pauline, proudly pointing out the updates she had made since purchasing the salon late last year.

"I like your beauty salon, Daphne. It's really quite nice." Pauline's voice softened, "And I especially like the name, "Daphne-Ray.""

"Thank you. I'm glad I have my own business, although it's really demanding at times."

"I'm sure it is." Pauline studied Daphne's face. "Where can we get a Coke or some ice cream?"

"Let's try Star Drug Store. It's just a few blocks away, so we can walk there. I'll grab my jacket."

Fifteen minutes later, the women were seated at a little round table in the back of the drug store sipping chocolate ice cream sodas.

"Remember the fun we had in Trenton, Daphne, when we explored the town? We nearly walked our feet off tromping through every other shop on the north side."

Daphne nodded. "We certainly enjoyed ourselves, didn't we?

Despite the way those eastern ladies looked down on us."

Pauline swallowed a drink of soda and then chuckled. "I'm sure they found our behavior strange too."

Daphne laughed. "I'll never forget the look on Mrs. Appledorn's face when we checked out of her boarding house a few days early." She took a sip of her soda before asking, "Is John still in Italy?"

"Yes."

"Do you hear much from him?"

"No. He doesn't have time to write often and when he does send a letter, it's usually brief."

"Hello Daphne." Daphne felt a hand gently rest on her shoulder. She looked up into the face of Inez Dulin, a customer from the Ione Beauty Salon. Daphne didn't know the woman well, but she remembered her quiet, sweet personality.

"Hello, Inez."

"I just wanted to tell you how sorry I am, honey, about the loss of your husband."

"Thank you." Daphne reached up and squeezed the woman's hand.

The woman looked across at Pauline, nodded a silent greeting, then turned and walked away quickly.

Pauline looked shaken. "Does this happen often, Daphne?"

Daphne nodded. "My friends and customers want to express their sympathy. I understand and appreciate it *now*. But for the first few months following Raymond's death, it was hard to even hear his name and not fall apart." Her voice trailed off. "I guess I've grown a little stronger."

Pauline stared into her soda glass, stirring the melting ice cream with a straw. "Oh Daphne, I can't imagine what these last six months have been like for you." When she looked up, her eyes were brimming with tears. "Raymond was a good, kind-hearted man with such a likeable personality. We will all miss him."

Daphne maintained her composure as the counter boy approached their table with a sales ticket. She reached for it, but Pauline got it first. "My treat."

"Thank you," Daphne said quietly. "You know, Pauline, this is the craziest thing, but I just keep hoping the Army made a mistake about Raymond's death. I mean, I still look through the mail, almost expecting there'll be a letter from the Government apologizing for their terrible mistake, telling me Raymond is still alive. Or that maybe one day I'll just turn around and there he'll be, like the day we met."

After a stretch of silence, Pauline gently placed a hand on Daphne's arm. "Oh, honey, I wouldn't get your hopes up."

Daphne looked down at her hands now folded on the table top. "I know it's ridiculous to have such thoughts, but I just can't keep them away."

40

April 12, 1945

It was almost four-thirty in the afternoon. Daphne crossed out the next few hours in her appointment book and then reached for her handbag. Her last customer had cancelled fifteen minutes earlier and she could leave for the day. She planned to stop by the LeMar Shop on her way home.

"Enjoy the beautiful weather, Daphne," said Mary Francis as she added a handful of combs to the sterilizing machine.

"I will. Bye girls." Daphne shut the door of the salon and headed down the flight of stairs and out the front door of the Heflin Building. She turned left and a few paces later opened the door to the LeMar Shop. Lena Crooks stood at the back of the store talking with a customer.

"Hi, Daphne," she called. "I'll be with you in a minute."

"Take your time, Lena," Daphne called back as she began rummaging through some discounted toddler clothes spread across the off-season sale table. Fingering a pink and white baby bonnet with intricately laced flowers, Daphne couldn't help but wonder how much fun it would have been to shop for her own son or daughter. But sadly, there would never be any Kelley babies.

Lena walked up and interrupted her thoughts. "It's good to see you, Daphne. Did you hear the news?"

Daphne's eyes became watchful. "No. What news?"

"President Roosevelt passed away," replied the older woman somberly. "An announcement was made on the radio just a few minutes ago."

"Oh, no," Daphne cried. "When did he die?"

"Sometime after one o'clock this afternoon. He was at his cottage in Warm Springs, Georgia. With all the rumors about his declining health, you would think this wouldn't be such a shock, but it is."

Daphne agreed. "I guess Vice President Truman will take over now." After more than twelve years of hearing "President Roosevelt this" and "President Roosevelt that," "President *Truman*" would sound strange, Daphne thought to herself.

"How are you doing, Daphne?" Lena asked quietly.

"Okay, I guess," Daphne replied casually as she pushed her thoughts aside. "I'm looking for a present for my friend's baby boy."

"Oh? How old is the child?"

Daphne thought for a moment. "He'll soon be two months old."

"Come this way." Lena led Daphne to a long row of shelves overflowing with neatly arranged piles of newborn outfits, underclothing, socks, booties, bibs, and a few plush toys. The women examined one stack after another, intent on comparing styles, sizes, and colors. Finally Daphne settled on two romper outfits, one medium blue and the other mint green and yellow plaid. She also selected matching booties.

"Feel this teddy bear, Daphne." Lena rubbed the downy-like bit of fluff against her friend's cheek. "Feels almost like a ball of cotton, doesn't it?"

Daphne reached for the little stuffed animal. "You're sure a good saleslady, Lena," she murmured. "I'm sure baby Steven will love it. Just add it to my purchases."

"Who is this little guy anyway?" Lena asked as she boxed and wrapped the outfits, booties, and toy.

Daphne explained how years earlier she had accompanied Steven's mother Mamie to a Sunday school picnic and subsequently was introduced to Raymond. She told Lena she and Raymond had stood up with Jim and Mamie Gates at their wedding and had been friends through the years.

Lena listened attentively as she topped off the brightly gift-wrapped box with a bow. "Well, please tell Mamie to stop by the store sometime, Daphne. I'd like to offer her the special discount I give for 'first-time mamas.'"

"Oh, Lena. That is nice of you." Daphne hugged her friend and collected her package.

"Let's make plans to meet for dinner sometime soon, Daphne."

Nodding, Daphne smiled as she headed out the door. "I'll check my calendar and give you a call. Bye, now."

Daphne walked home, allowing the warm sunshine to penetrate her body and lift her spirits. Ten minutes later, she was at the door of the little house on Green Street.

Maggie was standing in the kitchen staring out the window when Daphne walked in.

"Did you hear about President Roosevelt, Mother?"

Maggie turned around. "Yes. Mr. Byroads stopped by a few minutes ago and told us." She handed Daphne an envelope. "You received some mail today, dear. Looks like it may be another letter from that soldier friend of Raymond's."

Daphne's heart pounded as she took the envelope from her mother's hand. She headed for her bedroom and tore open the envelope from William Hicks. The man's vivid description of Raymond's final battle brought an end to any illusions that her husband had somehow survived. She read further:

However, the enemy's strength was greater than anticipated, having at least three tanks, a half-track with a flame thrower, an undetermined amount of infantry supported by mortars, and machine guns. The tanks had evidently been covering the road blocks but when we started our attack, they moved into position to cover the part of town we were entering. They opened fire on us with machine guns and Raymond, who was carrying the radio for the company commander, was hit in the shoulder and upper forearm. The wound was a painful one, but not fatal. As Raymond and the company commander were leading the attack, the medic was some twenty or thirty yards farther back. He was called up front immediately to give Raymond first aid. The Germans were trying to zero in on us with mortars and before the medic could complete the first aid and get Raymond out of the way, a mortar shell hit in a tree practically over their heads. A piece of shrapnel hit Raymond just over the heart, killing him instantly. I'm sure Raymond could have gone to the back of the line after he was hit, but he was never one to take the easy way out. Even though wounded, he stayed at his post and paid the supreme price that those whom he loved might live in freedom and in peace. May God grant that he died not in vain.

I hope I have done justice to him and have told you the things you most wanted to know. I'm sure I've fallen short of what I really intended to convey to you. However, try to read between the lines and get the real meaning that I in my very ignorance have been unable to impart to you. I must admire you in the stand you've taken in that grief and bitterness cannot bring him back. I'm sure time will eventually soften the shock of losing him and leave pride as the predominant feeling, with a spirit of greater depth, rather than one broken with despair. May God give you strength to endure.

Yes, I remember the picture I gave Raymond. He gave me one of himself which I've sent to Eula. He used to have one of you that I admired very much; the one of you sitting on the running board of the car. Did you get it back? I wouldn't think of asking for that particular one for I know if you have it, it must have a lot of sentimental value to you, but if you have one like it or similar, I wish you'd send it to me. I have quite a collection of photos of my dear friends and relatives. I'd like very much to add one of you.

I'd like for you to continue to write to me and I'll promise not to wait so long to answer next time. If there's anything else you'd like to know, I'd be glad to tell you if I can.

Hoping to hear from you in the very near future.

Ever a friend, William

The tears flowed down her cheeks and pain compressed her heart as Daphne slowly folded the letter and returned it to its envelope. Fused with her sorrow, however, was great pride in her husband's bravery and relief in knowing he had died instantly—at least physically anyway. His memory, Daphne was certain, would be with her forever.

YOU'LL NEVER KNOW, DEAR, HOW MUCH I LOVE YOU

41

Late April, 1945

Alone at the kitchen table, Daphne leafed through her scrapbook as she sipped a cup of coffee. Remembering the Purple Heart that had arrived posthumously a few weeks earlier, she hurried to her room to dig it out of her dresser drawer. Tenderly carrying it to the kitchen, she placed the medal alongside the others in the scrapbook.

As she looked up from the book and out the window, she was struck by the brilliant shades of red, white, and yellow in her father's roses. She smiled as she considered how faithfully he loved and tended the pretty flowers. They were truly his pride and joy.

Her thoughts again centered on Raymond. She thought of the deep love that had blossomed between her and her husband, and how it was like the pure, perfect beauty of the roses. *Oh Raymond*, she sighed, *why did God take you away so soon?* As she turned a page in the book, words began to form in her mind that begged to be written down. Using white ink, she wrote carefully onto the black pages of the scrapbook:

When You Come Home

A Rose Between God and Me

God gave to my keeping, a Rose,
Only He could make one so fine.
And the memory of it still glows,
Within this heart of mine.

It was in full bloom,
When He came to reclaim
My Rose for His garden above;
And I thank thee God for the joy of having
Had this Rose to love.

Though Raymond's body had been laid to rest in a military cemetery in Epinal, France, Daphne yearned for a local memorial. A few weeks earlier, she had arranged for a granite rectangle engraved with her husband's name to be delivered to Mount Tabor Cemetery in Fayette, a small town southeast of Lebanon. She now felt a strong desire to visit the cemetery to see if the stone had been delivered.

Daphne walked into the living room. Her mother was standing quietly by the window, observing the outside world. Daphne came up behind her and slipped her arm around the older woman's thin waist.

"What are you looking at, Mother?"

Maggie tucked a loose strand of gray hair behind her ear and nodded toward the tree in the front yard. "I'm just watching those two pretty little redbirds take turns darting back and forth between the trees. It's so good to hear the birds singing again and see the leaves starting to bud out once more. Goodness, it's been a long winter, hasn't it Daphne?"

Daphne understood exactly how her mother felt. It was a welcome treat to feel the warmth of the sun again. "It sure has been, Mother. And I'm certainly glad spring is finally here. Dad's roses seem more colorful this year than they have been in a long time."

Maggie nodded. "Oh my, yes. And he's already had to prune them quite a bit." She turned to face her daughter. "I see you've got your pocketbook with you. Are you headed out?"

"I'm going to drive out to the cemetery. I'll be back before long."

"Do you want me to come with you?"

Daphne started to shake her head but reconsidered. "Actually, it *would* be nice to have some company." She looked around. "Where's Dad? He might want to come too."

Both women smiled at the muffled sounds coming from the back bedroom. "I'm putting on my shoes, ladies. I'll be ready in a minute."

Arriving in the quiet little village of Fayette minutes later, Daphne steered the car through the graveyard gates. She helped her parents from the car and they walked slowly across the uneven ground and around the other tombstones to an open space next to the family plot. There stood the shiny new stone, its pretty rose tint sparkling in the late afternoon sunlight.

Daphne's breath caught in her throat and for a while she couldn't speak. Finally, she managed, "It's beautiful, isn't it?"

Maggie placed a hand on her daughter's arm and gave it a gentle squeeze. "It sure is, honey."

Bending down, the young widow tenderly placed some roses from her father's flower bed beside the monument. She read the inscription to herself:

Raymond R. Kelley, 1922 – 1944.
Killed in France September 10, 1944
Erected in loving memory by his wife

When You Come Home

Rising to her feet, Daphne stood still with her eyes closed and embraced the quiet. When she finally spoke, her voice trembled. "I still can't believe he's never coming back." She breathed a long sigh. "I know he's with the Lord, but I miss him so much."

Albert laid a comforting hand on her shoulder. "We all miss him, honey, but *he's* having the time of his life."

Daphne stood still as his words penetrated her grief. She thought of her dear, sweet husband forever freed from the chaotic, war-ravaged world. Was he up there right now talking and laughing with Jesus? Singing his favorite hymns? Leading a choir of angels in song? She could only imagine.

Finally, like a little girl, she linked arms with her father and mother. Thinking of Raymond's joy, she didn't feel the need to linger.

"Let's go home."

42

May 1, 1945

The music on the radio accompanied the gentle hum of the hair dryer inside the Daphne-Ray Beauty Shop. Daphne had allowed herself a few minutes to prop her feet up while her customer, Pearl Jackson, finished drying. As she idly flipped through the May issue of *Photoplay* magazine, the shop door swung open and Barbara Tanselle and Mary Francis Mohr walked through.

Daphne looked up and smiled. "How was lunch, ladies?"

Mary Francis grimaced. "I had the daily special at Wheelers. It was too spicy. Guess I should have ordered what Barbara had."

"What'd you have, Barbara?" asked Daphne, hoping it was more exotic than her own cheese sandwich.

"Chicken and dumplings, and were they ever good. Just like my grandma makes." Barbara flopped down on a nearby dryer chair.

Daphne was just about to remind the girl that her next appointment was due at any time when Mary Francis spoke up. "You should have come with us, Daphne." She walked over to her booth and glanced down at her open appointment book. "It's really nice outside and the walk would have been good for you." Mary Francis frowned at her boss. "You work too hard."

Daphne laid her movie magazine aside. "It's not going to hurt me to miss one meal. I'll make up for it tomorrow."

"Hey, what's that guy talking about on the radio?" Barbara asked.

Daphne stilled. The radio commentator was saying something about Adolph Hitler. She hurried over and turned up the volume. Through the static, the ladies heard:

Let me repeat . . . Germany has announced that
Adolph Hitler has committed suicide. His body
and the body of his long-time fiancée, Eva Braun,
were discovered yesterday in Hitler's Berlin bunker.
More details to follow on the regular broadcast.

After a few moments of silence, Daphne turned back to the women. "Did I hear that right? Hitler killed himself?"

"Yes, you heard it right." Mary Francis' face showed her shock at the announcement.

"I'm glad he's dead!" exclaimed Barbara. "He was a monster."

Daphne nodded in silent agreement. How could anyone be sad to hear that news? Surely the world would be better off without this evil man, and surely his demise would hasten the war's end.

Indeed, only a few days later, on May 7th, Germany surrendered and May 8th was declared "V-E Day" for Victory in Europe. The newspapers read, "After nearly six years of war in Europe and after tens of millions have died, the war is over at last!"

It was about one o'clock in the afternoon when Mamie Gates walked into the beauty shop.

"Hello, Mamie," Daphne said as she walked over to greet her friend. "I am so glad to see you."

The women hugged and then Mamie pulled back. "I'm sorry I had to cancel my appointment last month, Daphne. I wasn't quite ready to leave the baby yet."

Daphne nodded. "I understand. I hope you brought pictures of him."

"Well, of course." Mamie opened her wallet and together they pored over the black and white photos of baby Steven.

"He looks like you, Mamie." Daphne observed as she examined a picture of the baby nestled in his mother's arms.

"Do you think so?" Mamie sounded surprised. "Most people say he resembles his daddy."

"Well, he's precious either way." Daphne returned the pictures to Mamie and handed her the wrapped box. "Here's a little something for Steven from the LeMar Shop. You can open it when you get home."

"Oh, Daphne, you didn't have to get him anything."

"I enjoyed shopping for him. It gave me an excuse to visit with Lena and look at all the adorable baby clothes she sells." Daphne ushered Mamie over to the shampoo sink. "Let's get started."

The women chatted as Daphne wrapped her friend's hair into pin curls and added permanent solution to set the wave. Two hours later, Mamie studied her reflection in the mirror. "This is much better, Daphne, and the curly style should be easy to maintain."

"Good. Taking care of a two-month-old baby probably doesn't leave much time for standing in front of the mirror." Daphne smiled at her friend. "And I know how you love to primp." Whisking off the cape from Mamie's shoulders, she declared, "All done."

After promising to have supper at the Gates' farm the following week, Daphne closed the door behind Mamie. A quick glance at the clock confirmed it was only three o'clock, nearly an hour until her next appointment. Daphne walked to the back of the room, poured a cup of coffee, and sat down. She picked up *The Lebanon Reporter* and began to read. News of the victory in Europe filled the entire front page. With deep relief, she realized peace would finally return to the nation. The soldiers who were fortunate enough to have survived the war would come home and healing would begin.

"Did you hear me, Daphne?"

Startled, Daphne looked up. "What?"

Mary Francis was spraying a sink full of hairbrushes. "I've called your name twice, but you seemed lost in your thoughts."

"I'm sorry." Daphne heard a roar of voices outside and put down the paper. "What's going on out there?"

Mary Francis shook her head. "I don't know. Will you go look?"

Daphne moved from her chair and hurried over to the second-floor window. The large front-facing window was slightly ajar, so she cranked it open all the way, allowing the sounds from the street below to fill the room. She couldn't believe the scene that met her eyes.

"Mary Francis, you've got to see this." Daphne grabbed the sides of the window and leaned out further. Her voice became fainter. "People are gathered on the sidewalks and in the streets. They're singing and waving little American flags. They're even throwing confetti."

Mary Francis was at her side immediately. The woman's mouth flew open in astonishment. "Oh my goodness, look at all the people. There must be hundreds of them down there."

Daphne pointed towards the jail. "Look over there. Someone just set off fireworks."

After a while, Mary Francis turned to her friend, her words soft. "Do you want to go down, Daphne?"

A touch of sadness shadowed Daphne's face as she continued to watch the happy throng of partiers below. "No, I don't think I can. The view from up here is close enough for me. What about you?"

Mary Francis wrapped an arm around Daphne's waist. "I think I'll stay up here too."

A few minutes later, Daphne stretched out her arm. "Oh, look. See those servicemen walking towards the courthouse steps? I'll bet they just got off the noon train. Everyone's running to greet them."

Mary Francis nodded her head as she watched. "The soldiers must be thrilled to be home."

A lump formed in Daphne's throat as she thought of Jim Stout, John Cartmill, and Clinton Shaw. Raymond's buddies would finally be reunited with their wives and families. What a joyful homecoming awaited them. And Jack would be coming home. She couldn't wait to hug him and assure herself that he was indeed okay.

Both women kept their eyes glued to the outpouring of gaiety and patriotism exhibited in the streets and sidewalks below. "This is wonderful," Daphne murmured. "I wonder if other towns around the country are celebrating like this."

"I wouldn't be surprised."

For a long time, the women stood side-by-side watching, mesmerized by the goings-on below. Finally, Daphne leveled a look at one friend who could *really* understand the words she was about to say.

"Thank you, God. It's finally over."

43

Late July, 1945

Her feet tired and energy sapped from a long day in the hot, stuffy beauty shop, Daphne plodded home beneath the late afternoon sun. She couldn't wait to kick off her shoes and collapse onto the couch. As she opened the front screen door of the Abston house, however, she was stopped by her mother's voice. "Daphne, come in here, please."

Maggie was standing against the counter wiping her flour-dusted hands on her apron. She pointed toward a small brown bundle on the kitchen table. "This package came in the mail for you today, dear."

"Oh? I wonder what it is." Daphne hurried over to the table.

Maggie's expression clouded as she gently patted her daughter's shoulder. "It's from the United States Government," she said softly. "So maybe you'd better sit down."

Sitting on the kitchen chair, thankful her mother left the room, Daphne pulled the package onto her lap and ripped it open. Out spilled Raymond's now dilapidated billfold and its contents. Struggling to maintain her composure, Daphne examined the familiar items her husband had so cherished and kept with him—a strand of her own red hair—pictures of her and Raymond and his sister Mary—Raymond's driver's license.

Lifting the inside flap of the wallet, Daphne gingerly pulled out the poem, *When You Come Home*, that she had sent Raymond nearly two years before. It was stained with blood—the blood from her husband's mortal wounds.

Daphne's fragile body convulsed with long pent-up sobs and she cried for some time. She could sense the presence of her parents just outside the kitchen door, but she was grateful they were leaving her alone with her grief. Tender words and warm hugs could never soothe her broken heart on a day like this.

When the tears finally stopped, Daphne stood, composed herself and wiped her eyes. The wallet was in shreds, but she had no intention of discarding something so dear of her beloved soldier's. Instead, she held it to her cheek. The blood stains were part of him. The only part she could keep.

Albert and Maggie appeared in the doorway. "Are you all right, Daphne?" Albert inquired quietly.

Her voice was shaky. "The Army returned these things along with Raymond's wallet." Daphne gestured toward the items strewn across the table and then held up a newspaper clipping. "Here's the poem I sent him."

As Albert walked over to pick up the now stained and weathered piece of paper, Maggie steadied herself against the door frame. "I remember when you sent that poem to Raymond." Her eyes glistened behind wire-framed glasses. "It seems like ages ago."

Daphne nodded, the tears welling up again. "I miss him so much,

Mom."

Albert patted his daughter's shoulder. "There, there, honey. We know you do." He pulled a handkerchief from his pocket and offered it to Daphne.

"Thanks, Dad." After wiping her eyes, Daphne gathered the mementos and headed to her bedroom. Once inside her room, she picked up her scrapbook and glued the items, one-by-one, onto the pages.

Late that night Daphne crawled into bed, suddenly overcome with fatigue. She felt the need to pray, but couldn't concentrate. Her thoughts fluttered like heartbeats and were washed away by big, salty tears with no end. As she turned over on her side, trying to come to grips with the overwhelming sadness, her prayer was simple. *Lord please help me bear this grief.* Her thoughts then took hold of a scripture, the fifth verse of the Psalm 30:

For His anger endureth but a moment; in his favour is life: weeping may endure for a night, but joy cometh in the morning.

Her eyes closed in sleep.

Daphne kept the scrapbook by her side through the night. She restlessly tossed and turned and was troubled by many random thoughts, but for some reason her thoughts kept returning to the night when she and the girls from the Ione Salon had gone to see *Since You Went Away* in Indianapolis. Something nagged at the edges of her memory, something she couldn't quite grasp or clarify.

Dawn wasn't far off when Daphne finally rose from her bed. She walked over to the dresser, but couldn't find her hairbrush. Opening a drawer, she found the brush, but she also saw the hated yellow telegram she had received informing her that Raymond was dead. It should go in the scrapbook, she thought. As she carried it to the bed, she unfolded and read the note again.

...REPORT NOW RECEIVED STATES HE WAS KILLED IN ACTION ON TEN SEPTEMBER...

Her mouth went dry. Why hadn't she realized it before? Factoring in the time difference, the moment she had been visited in the night by Raymond, he had most likely just gone to be with the Lord. Daphne sat down numbly on the mattress.

Had Raymond been on his way to heaven when he stopped for one last precious moment, one last time to say good-bye and assure her of his love? Or had God sent Raymond back to her, ever so briefly, to comfort her with His divine and eternal love?

As morning light broke across her bed and washed over the mementos of her life with Raymond, Daphne pulled the blood-stained poem from the scrapbook and read it again.

When you come home, come home once more to me.
It is unlikely, dear that I shall be
Articulate. The words I've wanted so
To say, I'll try in vain to speak, I know;
I shall reach blindly for you, stricken dumb
With swift and aching joy when you come.

Or if my tongue find utterance at all
It will be commonplace and trivial.
But you will understand and, oh, once more,
I'll feel your hand laid lightly on my hair
As was your wont, smoothing it again

When You Come Home

And yet again. You'll lift my face and then
We shall forget all else. You'll hold me fast.
When you come home, Come home to me at last!

She held the poem to her cheek, aware of the delicate stationery as surely as she had felt the rough fabric of Raymond's uniform and the beating of his heart.

He had kept his promise.

He had come home . . . home to her at last.

Epilogue

Saturday Evening, June 22, 1996

Daphne closed the scrapbook.

Neither of the women spoke for the longest time and the silence endured as Nancy held her mother's hand. Together they placed the book atop the others, the memories no longer buried, no longer hidden.

When Nancy looked out the window, she realized the sun was setting. It had been a long day.

A long day well spent.

CPSIA information can be obtained at www.ICGtesting.com
Printed in the USA
LVOW120706071211

258201LV00001B/10/P